Victorious Bible Curriculum

THE BEGINNING (PART 1 OF 9)
God created a home for mankind, and placed us in it to tend and guard it as His image. When we rebelled, God promised a seed of the woman to one day restore creation — and preserved that seed when our violence filled the world.

THE PATRIARCHS (PART 2 OF 9)
God chose Abraham to be the custodian of the line through which the promised redeemer would come. Abraham's grandson Jacob became the father of the twelve tribes of Israel, a nation that would bless the whole earth.

THE EXODUS (PART 3 OF 9)
For 400 years, God grew Jacob's tiny family into a nation. Through Moses, He released them from slavery to give them a new home. Despite the faithless first generation's rebellion, their children would inherit the promised land.

CONQUEST AND JUDGMENT (PART 4 OF 9)
Under Joshua, the children of the exodus conquered the promised land. After they settled in, they fell into idolatry and suffered under foreign domination. Time after time, they needed God's deliverance through a head-crushing judge.

THE KINGDOM OF ISRAEL (PART 5 OF 9)
God used Israel's first kings, the vacillating Saul and the head-crusher David, to give Israel peace. Solomon built a prosperous kingdom, which then split and fell into idolatry. After 70 years' exile in Babylon, God restored them to the land.

THE COMING OF THE MESSIAH (PART 6 OF 9)
The long wait for the serpent-crushing redeemer came to an end with the birth of Jesus of Nazareth. Raised in Galilee and baptized in the Jordan, He began to proclaim the kingdom of God and demonstrate God's love and power.

THE MINISTRY OF JESUS (PART 7 OF 9)
The blind could see, the sick were healed, the dead raised. The kingdom of God was truly at hand. But the leaders of Israel rejected the One God had sent to save them from their sins and deliver them into God's kingdom.

JESUS' FINAL DAYS (PART 8 OF 9)
On Thursday, before His arrest, Jesus ate one final meal with His disciples. Then He was arrested, beaten, falsely accused, tried, convicted and crucified. But death could not hold Him and the grave could not contain Him.

THE BEGINNING OF THE CHURCH (PART 9 OF 9)
After His resurrection, Jesus' followers received the power of the Holy Spirit to disciple the nations of the world, baptizing them and teaching them all that Jesus had said. Christ's body grew and began to crush the enemy's head under her feet.

Copyright © 2016 by Joe Anderson and Tim Nichols

All rights reserved
Printed in the United States of America
First Edition

No part of this book may be reproduced in any form or by any electronic or mechanical means, including information storage and retrieval systems, except for brief quotations in printed reviews, without the prior permission of the author.

Unless otherwise indicated, all Scripture quotations are taken from the New King James Version®. Copyright © 1982 by Thomas Nelson, Inc. Used by permission. All rights reserved.

Scripture quotations marked (NIV) are taken from the Holy Bible, New International Version®, NIV®. Copyright © 1973, 1978, 1984, 2011 by Biblica, Inc.™ Used by permission of Zondervan. All rights reserved worldwide. www.zondervan.com The "NIV" and "New International Version" are trademarks registered in the United States Patent and Trademark Office by Biblica, Inc.™

Author's translation or paraphrase indicated by an asterisk after the reference.

Illustrations by Gustave Doré
Colorized and modified by William Britton

Praise for Headwaters Bible Curriculum

These lessons are not just a way to teach the Bible to middle school kids. As I read the lessons, I found both my head and my heart irresistibly engaged. Joe and Tim have opened the grace and truth of God's Word in a way that seriously lifts us towards Christ while nudging us outward towards the world. I recommend these studies for both devotional and motivational reading!

Dave Cheadle, President of the Rocky Mountain Classis, Reformed Church of America

While I have spent quite a bit of time studying the Bible myself, I find your ideas and themes to be real food for thought and they help tie together much of the story God is telling throughout... I've already talked with people about your curriculum and have recommended they look into it for their own families. I can't loan out my copy for their perusal, because I'm using it everyday!

Linda Kidder, Home Educator, Colorado

I LOVE THIS BOOK!!!! We're just finishing up the Garden narrative. We've had such fruitful discussions—I have been pleased with it in every way. In fact, I'm hoping our church will start using it. I haven't had any problems or difficulties using the curriculum, I ONLY have good things to say about it. In fact, I'm in danger of writing in all caps I'm so enthusiastic about it.

Leah Robinson, Home Educator, Texas

I am really enjoying having this resource to work from and steer our lessons!

Christy Johnson, Bible Teacher, Bingham Academy, Ethiopia

Our family actually loves the curriculum. My children are in 5th and 8th grade and the content has suited both of their levels perfectly. To this point we hadn't found a curriculum that taught the Bible at such a detailed level that has also kept the kids engaged. We've had to slow down on the materials because otherwise they would be through them well before the school year is up. We are planning on buying the rest of the series.

Chris Turner, Home Educator, Colorado

How to Use This Book

This series of little manuals walks you through the biblical Story from end to end. Just read. Here are a few things you might want to keep in mind as you read through the Story.

- Try to love the characters. God does....
- The story is written in such a way as to make sin look stupid, but remember that the characters are all real people. No matter how stupid the choice, a real person actually looked at the options and then picked that particular one for reasons that seemed pretty good at the time. Nobody gets up in the morning and says, "I'm going to make stupid life choices that people will be mocking for centuries." Try to see it from their point of view. Ask yourself, "Why did this look like a good idea at the time?" That's how you learn to recognize temptations. It's easy to see sinful and stupid choices for what they are in hindsight, but in the moment it's often very hard. So learn to think through what these choices looked like from the inside, in the heat of the moment — you'll be amazed what you learn about yourself.
- Pay attention to the patterns. We'll point out a bunch of them as we go through the Story, but try to spot them yourself, too. If you can learn to read the Word and see the patterns in the Story, you will become able to read the world around you and see the patterns in the story God is telling right now.
- Each lesson comes with a psalm. The psalms provide us with another lens through which to look at the Story, and God has a lot to teach us that way. Sometimes we've given you an activity that will help integrate the psalm with that episode in the Story. Other times, we've just given you the psalm, and we're going to let you fill in the blanks. Read over the psalm a few times, then go into the lesson and see what comes to you. You'll be surprised what you can learn.
- As with any book that talks about Scripture, don't necessarily take our word for anything. Imagine you're sitting in a living room or around a campfire with us, and we're just talking about the Story. You're free to disagree, correct, challenge our understanding. The Word is the authority, not us — so grab your Bible and look things up yourself.

You'll find a section labeled "Activities" following the lesson. The point of this section is to immerse you as deeply in the Story as possible, through prayer, meditation on the Story, and other exercises. The "Evaluation" questions at the end of each lesson will help you to check your understanding of the material.

For Small Group Leaders
Have everyone in the group read the lesson ahead of time. Depending on how involved your group is, you can have them engage some or all of the activities, or you can save those for group time when you're together. The evaluation questions might serve as discussion starters if the conversation lags.

For Homeschoolers
Have your student read the lesson and complete the activities. (Some might be more appropriate as whole-family activities.) You can use the evaluation questions as a quiz or as discussion starters to check your student's comprehension of the lesson.

Table of Contents

Unit 5 The Exodus 7
    Lesson 5.1 Moses the Deliverer's Miraculous Birth and Meeting with God in Midian 9
    Lesson 5.2 Israel's Oppression and Yahweh's Defeat of the Egyptian Gods 17
    Lesson 5.3 The Passover and Israel's Escape from Egypt 27
    Lesson 5.4 The Red Sea Crossing and the Song of Moses 35
    Lesson 5.5 Israel Developed a Habit of Complaint; God Continued to Provide 43
    Lesson 5.6 Israel Distanced Herself from God and His Prophet 51
    Lesson 5.7 Moses Met with God and Received the Law 57
    Lesson 5.8 True Worship in the Tabernacle and False Worship of the Golden Calf 65
    Lesson 5.9 Priestly Law: God Separated Israel as a Nation of Priests 73
    Lesson 5.10 Israel's Rebellion at Kadesh Barnea 83

UNIT 5: THE EXODUS

In Egypt, God blessed Israel so greatly that the Egyptians were afraid and enslaved them, but God heard their cries and provided Moses, miraculously preserving and preparing him through childhood. A premature effort at protecting a Hebrew slave resulted in Moses killing an Egyptian, and Moses fled to Midian. At a well in Midian he saved seven shepherdesses from men who were harassing them; Moses ended up marrying one of these shepherdesses and living with her father Jethro. After 40 years, God appeared to Moses in a burning bush on Mt. Horeb (Sinai) while Moses was shepherding Jethro's sheep. God told Moses he was chosen to deliver Israel, overrode his initial objections and excuses, and sent him to Egypt with his brother Aaron to assist him.

Moses confronted Pharaoh with God's demand to release Israel, but instead Pharaoh increased Israel's burden. Although God did signs and wonders through Aaron and Moses, Pharaoh hardened his heart. God then brought plagues on Egypt, each one targeting the domain of a specific Egyptian god. God crushed the head (rulership) of nine gods in turn, bringing Egypt to total destruction and ruin. Still Pharaoh refused, and God brought one final plague. In order to be delivered through the plague, Israel had to perform the Passover ceremony. As the angel of death killed all the firstborn sons, he passed over the Israelite homes marked with the blood of the Passover lamb, and in this way God delivered Israel through the plague and out of the land of Egypt. God led the Israelites to the Red Sea where they were surrounded by mountains and trapped between the sea and the Egyptian army. Israel complained against the Lord, but He opened the sea and led them through the waters, while the Egyptians who pursued them were drowned. Finally free from Egypt, Israel praised God on the shores of the Red Sea.

To teach Israel to rely on Him, God led them into situations where they needed Him to provide the very basics of life: water, food, and physical protection. They responded in each case by complaining that He was trying to kill them in the wilderness. God continued to provide, but warned them against continuing to complain. In the wilderness Israel had the opportunity to have a close relationship with Moses, God's prophet, but they generated so many conflicts that Moses couldn't handle them all and had to institute a bureaucracy. When God led the nation to Sinai, He spoke the Ten Commandments directly to Israel, but they repeated the mistake, choosing to use Moses and the Law as intermediaries rather than relating to God directly. Still seeking relationship with them, God had them build the tabernacle, a portable Mt. Sinai and garden of Eden where His presence dwelt. Even as God was teaching all these things to Moses, Israel was rebelling and worshiping a golden calf (a common idol of the surrounding nations).

God disciplined Israel's rebellion, but continued His plan to make them a nation of priests to the world, giving them special instructions that would mark them as distinct from the other nations, teach them how to approach God properly, and guide them in remembering Him and His plan over time. From Sinai He led them up to Kadesh Barnea to go into the land that He had promised to Abraham so long ago, but they refused to enter, saying that the inhabitants were too strong and would kill them.

LESSON 5.1

Moses the Deliverer's Miraculous Birth and Meeting with God in Midian

UNIT 5

THE STORY

Lesson Theme - God formed and called Moses to be Israel's deliverer.

Moses was created by God to be the seed who crushed the head of the serpent Pharaoh; he was to be a savior for Israel from slavery and death in a foreign land. From his miraculous salvation at birth to when he met God at Sinai, Moses' life was a journey of preparation to be the deliverer. Of course, Moses didn't see it and thought God had chosen the wrong guy... but God knew what He was doing.

Israel had been in Egypt for quite some time now; Joseph and the Pharaoh who knew him had both died. The new Pharaoh was threatened by Israel because they had grown greatly in number, and he was afraid they would ally with Egypt's enemies and defeat them. He enslaved the Israelites, then ordered that all the newborn Hebrew sons must be killed, but Israel continued to multiply (Exod 1).

In the Bible, God's deliverers commonly had miraculous births (Isaac, Samson, Samuel, Jesus, etc.). Often, they were born to barren women or even a virgin. In this story, Moses was born at a time when all newborn boys were supposed to be put to death. Instead of trying to protect her son, Moses' mother put him in God's care, placing him in a small "ark" (think Noah's ark) among the reeds of the river (Exod 2:3). An ark on the water is a picture of baptism (death and resurrection). Moses was then miraculously saved by a daughter of Pharaoh (Exod 2:5-10). She should have had him killed, but instead protected him

OVERVIEW

Israel's initially good experience in Egypt had turned to misery and God wanted to deliver them. He chose Moses for this task and miraculously preserved and prepared him even as a child. When Moses grew up, he was forced to flee from Pharaoh after killing an Egyptian who was beating a Hebrew. Moses ended up in Midian where he saved the seven daughters of Jethro from shepherds who were harassing them at the well. He married one of Jethro's daughters and lived in Jethro's house. One day, as Moses was shepherding Jethro's sheep at Mt. Horeb (Sinai), God appeared to him in a burning bush and told him to deliver Israel out of Egypt. Moses objected, saying that he wasn't qualified, but God would have none of it. Moses was a born deliverer, now called by God to deliver His people.

SOURCE MATERIAL

- Exodus 1:1-4:17
- Psalm 65
- Proverbs 29:25

and raised him. Here, in the first part of Moses' life, God was preparing Moses to lead Israel; God was protecting him and guiding his life. Additionally, Moses' life prefigured what would happen to Israel later on. Just as Moses went through a death and resurrection (baptism) in the reeds of the Nile, Israel would later go through a death

Unit 5: The Exodus

OBJECTIVES

Feel...

- sadness for Israel, especially for the women whose sons were being killed by the Egyptians.
- gratitude for God's miraculous salvation of Moses from death in the river.
- awe at how God guided Moses' life to prepare him to be a deliverer.
- a sense of humility that God chooses the lowly for great tasks.

Understand...

- that Moses is the head-crushing seed character in this story (even though he is not in the seed-line).
- that as head of Israel, Moses prefigured Israel's later experiences in the exodus.
- that Moses showed natural aptitude for delivering Israel, even if he lacked wisdom in his approach (as shown by killing the Egyptian).
- that even though Moses objected to it, God's plan to use him still went forward.
- that God gave Moses power over the serpent and disease, demonstrating to Israel that He had called Moses to battle against Pharaoh.
- that Moses functioned in a priestly way for the nation of Israel.

Apply this understanding by...

- observing what skills and passions God is cultivating in your life.
- imagining what responsibilities God might call you to in the future based on how God is preparing your now.

and resurrection in the Red Sea (also called the Sea of Reeds).

Moses was a born deliverer. He *wanted* to save Israel, but before he went to Midian and met with God at Sinai, he lacked the maturity and a proper relationship with God to do it. We see this demonstrated when Moses killed an Egyptian who was beating an Israelite (Exod 2:11-15). Moses had the right desire to deliver his people; God had created him for that job, but Moses' methods were all wrong.

Again, when Moses arrived in Midian, he played the role of deliverer, only this time more honorably. The priest of Midian had seven daughters who went to the well to get water for their father's flocks. Some shepherds came and drove the women away; Moses saw this injustice and protected the women as they drew their water (Exod 2:16-20). Notice the contrast here between Moses and Adam. In the garden of Eden, Adam betrayed his wife instead of protecting her. Here Moses, a seed of the woman, was protecting women. This is model behavior for a Christ-like deliverer; and Moses ended up marrying one of these daughters (Exod 2:21-22). Isaac and Jacob's wives were both provided at a well, and now Moses met his wife at a well. We will see this theme of meeting a wife at a well repeated again.

So, Moses married and settled in Midian. Meanwhile, life was hard for the Israelites in Egypt. One day while Moses was shepherding Jethro's flocks, he came to Mt. Horeb, which is also known as Mt. Sinai, and God appeared to him there in a burning bush (Exod 3:1-3). Later, like Moses, Israel would leave Egypt; like Moses, they would wander in the wilderness; and again, like Moses, they would meet God at Mt. Sinai. This is how God prepares and trains leaders. God often

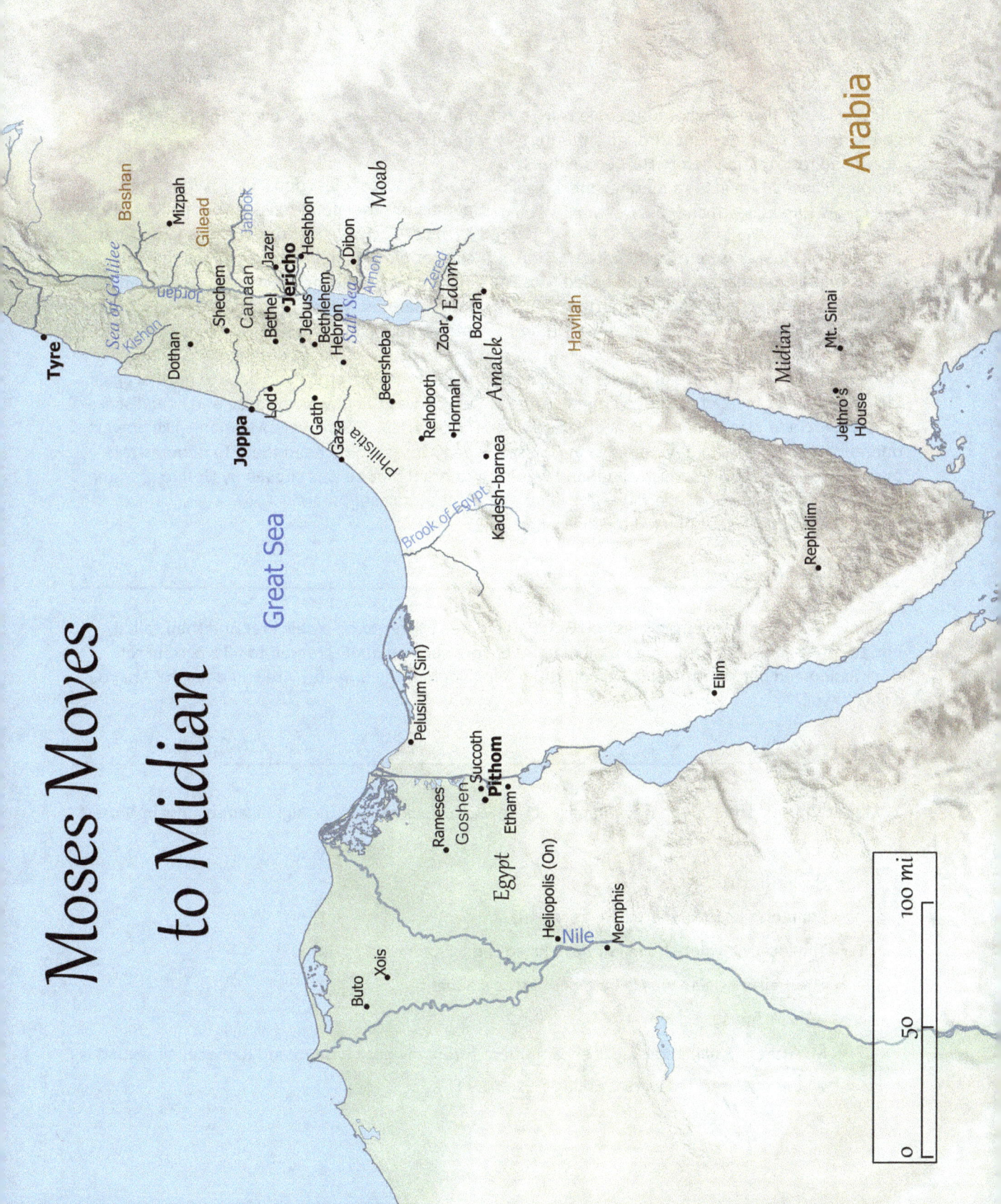

brings a leader through what his people will go through later. Jesus went through suffering, death and resurrection before His people did. His people followed Him in His suffering; and we also will follow Him in death and resurrection.

The story of Moses is often taught with the emphasis (rightly) on the fact that God called Moses *in spite* of his objections. This is important, but our main point here is *God's providential preparation* of Moses to be the deliverer for Israel so God could fulfill His promise of deliverance. The fact that Moses objected serves to emphasise that it was *God's* plan to deliver Israel that was operating; Moses didn't get veto rights in God's plan. Moses was a Levite (priestly line) and was simply called to obey God regarding His calling on his life. When Moses objected to God calling him, Moses was simply overstepping his priestly bounds.

One of Moses' objections was, "What if the people of Israel don't believe You really spoke to me?" God gave Moses two signs to prove to the people of Israel that he was the real thing. The first sign was the ability to turn his staff into a serpent, which represented power over the serpent (something Moses would need as a head-crusher). The second sign was the power to turn his hand leprous and back to normal again, which was the power to cause and heal disease (Exod 4:1-8). These were Messianic-like powers, and Moses would need them to demonstrate to Israel that he was chosen by God to fight the battle against Pharaoh.

APPLICATION

"Calling" is the big theme in this lesson. God had created Moses to be a deliverer and then called him to the task. God has a calling for all of us! We were each uniquely created to fill a certain role in the mission and purposes of God. Do you know what your calling is in life? Are you doing it? Are you doing it well?

ACTIVITIES

1. Map It: Moses' Life. On the map on page 11, mark the locations of the significant events in Moses' life.

- His birthplace
- Pharaoh's house (where he was raised)
- The location where he might have killed the Egyptian
- The well in Midian where he aided Jethro's daughters
- Jethro's house
- Mt. Horeb (Sinai) and Israel's encampment (probably near Pithom and Rameses since that is where the Israelites were working—Exod 1:11)

Lesson 5.1

Then draw a line representing Moses' travels to each of these places and his return trip to Egypt. Some of the locations are given on the map, others will require your imagination for placement.

2. Journal Time. God had prepared Moses to be the deliverer, but He didn't give him everything he needed; Moses still had to rely on God. Consider Moses' life and answer the following questions in the space below.

What natural gifts has God given you that He might use to fulfill His calling on your life? _____
_____
_____
_____
_____
_____
_____
_____

How has God used you in the past, and what do you think He might call you to do or be in the future?
_____
_____
_____
_____
_____
_____
_____
_____
_____
_____

Unit 5: The Exodus

What happens if God calls you to do something that requires abilities you don't have? Do you believe God can strengthen you to do what He has called you to do? _____
_____
_____
_____
_____
_____
_____
_____
_____
_____

EVALUATION

1. Why did Pharaoh enslave Israel? _____
_____
_____
_____

2. Write down three ways that God guided and prepared Moses to be a deliverer. _____
_____
_____
_____
_____
_____

3. Why did God plan to save Israel from Egypt? _____
_____
_____
_____
_____
_____

4. Why did Moses go to Midian? _____
_____
_____
_____
_____

5. Moses objected to God's calling on his life; was this right or wrong? Did God take Moses' objections seriously? _____
_____
_____
_____

6. What gifts did God give Moses to use as signs to prove that God had called him to the task of deliverance?_____
_____
_____

LESSON 5.2

Israel's Oppression and Yahweh's Defeat of the Egyptian Gods

THE STORY

Lesson Theme - Yahweh crushed the heads of the Egyptian gods.

The main point in this lesson is that Yahweh used the plagues to defeat the Egyptian gods. The words of Moses' father-in-law in response to Moses' report of Israel's exodus provide the key verse for this lesson: "Now I know that the LORD is greater than all other gods, for he did this to those who had treated Israel arrogantly" (Exod 18:11, NIV). This verse provides a helpful way to frame this lesson. The plagues were not just ways to make Pharaoh and the Egyptians hurt so that they might release Israel to worship Yahweh. They were *that;* but also, each plague was an attack by Yahweh against a different god or gods in Egypt.

After Moses had left Jethro's house, Aaron, following God's leading, met with Moses in the wilderness; Moses told Aaron all that God had instructed him to do (Exod 4:27-28). Then Moses and Aaron went to the elders of Israel and explained that the Lord was going to deliver them. They validated God's call with the signs the Lord had given Moses to do (turning his rod into a serpent and turning his hand leprous and back again). The people of Israel believed and worshiped God (Exod 4:29-31). Moses and Aaron then spoke to Pharaoh, telling him to release the people of Israel. Remember, however, that the Lord had said to Moses that He would harden Pharaoh's heart so that he would not release them (Exod 3:19). God was not just interested in bringing Israel out of Egypt and into the promised land; if that was all He wanted to do, He could have made Pharaoh release them right away. Instead, God wanted to show His power over the false gods in Egypt; in order to defeat the Egyptian gods, it was necessary to harden Pharaoh's heart.

OVERVIEW

God called Moses back to Egypt to deliver the nation of Israel out of slavery. Moses confronted Pharaoh who refused to let Israel go. Instead, Pharaoh increased the burden on the Israelites. After God reassured Moses that He would deliver Israel, Moses and Aaron went back to Pharaoh, and Aaron threw his rod down which turned into a serpent. Pharaoh's magicians were also able to perform this feat, but Aaron's rod devoured their rods. Still, Pharaoh hardened his heart and refused to release Israel. God then brought plagues on the land of Egypt; each plague was an attack against a specific god of the land. In this way, God crushed the heads of the Egyptian gods. The first nine of these plagues brought Egypt into total destruction and ruin.

SOURCE MATERIAL

- Exodus 4:18-10:29; 12:12; 18:11
- Psalm 105:26-45
- Proverbs 28:14
- *A Dictionary of Egyptian Gods and Goddesses* by George Hart

Unit 5: The Exodus

> **OBJECTIVES**
>
> **Feel...**
>
> - shock at the hardness of Pharaoh's heart as God brought the plagues against Egypt.
> - awe at God's power to bring destruction on Egypt.
> - gratitude that God used Moses even though Moses thought he couldn't do it.
>
> **Understand...**
>
> - that God Himself, through Moses and Aaron, was crushing the heads of the Egyptian gods.
> - which gods were defeated and how the plagues demonstrated power over each of these gods.
> - that Pharaoh hardened his heart again after each of the plagues.
> - that the land of Egypt, including its crops and livestock, was devastated by the plagues.
>
> **Apply this understanding by...**
>
> - determining if there are any areas in your life where, like Pharaoh, you are hardening your heart against God.
> - confessing any hardness in your heart towards God and seeking God's deliverance.

Consequently, when Moses and Aaron first went to Pharaoh to ask him to let the children of Israel go, it made things worse rather than better for the Israelites. Pharaoh demanded that they continue the same output of bricks, except now they had to collect their own straw (Exod 5:6-8). This was an impossible demand and gave the taskmasters an opportunity to beat the Israelites. Because of this increased oppression, the Israelites became angry with Moses and Aaron (Exod 5:21). Of course, Moses didn't like that the people were angry with him, so he spoke to God, and God reassured him that He would deliver Israel (Exod 6:1). Again Moses objected that he wasn't up to the task because he couldn't speak well. But Moses' weakness didn't matter; God was the one doing the delivering; Moses was simply called to obey (remember the previous lesson).

So Moses and Aaron went before Pharaoh a second time. This time, according to God's direction to Moses, Aaron threw his rod down on the ground, and it became a serpent (Exod 7:9). This was Yahweh's first challenge against the gods of Egypt. The cobra was a symbol of ruling authority in Egypt. Pharaoh was considered Egypt's highest god, and on his crown was a cobra poised to strike. Pharaoh is the serpent in this story, and Moses is the seed. By turning the rod into a serpent, Moses and Aaron were asking: who has more power, Yahweh, or the serpent-king? When Pharaoh saw Moses and Aaron turn the rod into a serpent, he called in his best sorcerers and they too turned their rods into serpents. These sorcerers had real power; their gods were not fake—they were demonic. They had real power, but their power was limited. Aaron and Moses, on the other hand, had the infinite power of God on their side. So Pharaoh's sorcery was no match for theirs—Aaron's rod consumed the serpents of Pharaoh's magicians (Exod 7:12). This was a prophecy of how the story would end; Yahweh has authority over the serpent; He would crush the heads of the Egyptian gods.

Not surprisingly, Pharaoh's heart was hardened further, and he did not let Israel go. So God began to bring plagues against Egypt, each one

worse than the last and each one targeted at an Egyptian god.

It's important that you understand what Egyptian worship was like. The major points are as follows: (1) Egyptian religion was polytheistic; their worship was directed toward multiple gods who were in control of various aspects of nature and were related to each other. (2) The universe was held together and in balance by a truth-order (*Ma'at*) that had been in place since creation. That order was sustained by every person in society participating in Egyptian religion; thus, there was great pressure to conform. (3) On the one hand, Pharaoh was considered human; on the other hand, he was among the greatest of the gods. He was the leader of religious worship in Egypt and was held in great esteem by the people. (4) There were many Egyptian gods, but some were more important than others. The really important gods included Ra, the sun god; Amun, the creator god and father of the Pharaohs; and Geb, the earth-god who blessed the Egyptians with crops and caused earthquakes.

In each of the plagues, Yahweh addressed himself to different Egyptian gods, demonstrating His power over them. In this way He crushed the heads of the gods of Egypt. The following paragraphs take a look at how each of the plagues was related to different gods in the Egyptian pantheon. In the next lesson we will look at the final plague (Passover) which was a direct attack on Pharaoh himself, thought to be the highest of the Egyptian gods.

In the first plague, God instructed Moses and Aaron to stand next to the Nile and speak to Pharaoh, then strike the water with the serpent-rod, and the Nile would turn into blood (Exod 7:19). The Nile was a source of life to the Egyptians; without its water they would be unable to grow crops, and their water supplies would be seriously lacking. Consequently, they worshiped the Nile in the form of the god Hapi: the spirit of the Nile in flood who was considered a life-giving god. To turn the Nile to blood was a direct attack on one of the most revered gods of Egypt.

In the second plague, God caused the Nile to bring forth an unreasonable number of frogs which made their way into people's homes and bedrooms and beds (Exod 8:3). This plague was an attack against the frog-headed goddess Heqet, one of the most ancient fertility goddesses in Egypt. She was associated with the abundance of frogs (though not unreasonably abundant) characteristic of the final stages of Nile flooding. These frogs were considered by the Egyptians a sign of the fertility of the Nile. In causing the Nile to produce an overabundance of these frogs, Yahweh was showing His power over Heqet by beating her at her own game and turning her blessing into a curse.

In the third plague, Moses struck the dust of the ground, and it became lice which inflicted the Egyptians (Exod 8:17). There is no known lice-god in the Egyptian pantheon, but there was a god of the earth known as Geb. Geb was responsible for the grain crops and for earthquakes (which were said to occur when he laughed). When Moses struck the ground and it turned to lice, he was striking Geb and showing power over him.

The fourth plague was an extension of the third. In the third, the land produced lice which attacked the people. In the fourth, Moses produced a great swarm of insects (perhaps of flies or some other insect; the Hebrew isn't clear). The land was then "corrupted because of the swarms" (Exod 8:24). In the third plague Geb

was overpowered; in the fourth plague Geb was attacked.

In the fifth plague, God sent pestilence on the cattle of Egypt (Exod 9:6). This was an attack on the great cow-headed goddess, Hathor. She was one of the most important, popular, and powerful deities in ancient Egypt and received direct worship from Pharaoh. Yahweh showed His power over this "mighty" deity by killing off most of the cattle in Egypt. This plague would have also been taken as a personal attack against Pharaoh himself.

In the sixth plague, Moses scattered ashes which became a dust in the land of Egypt and produced boils on all the Egyptians (Exod 9:10). This plague was most likely an attack on one or several of the gods of healing; Im-hotep and Sekhmet are two of these gods.

Unit 5: The Exodus

In the seventh plague, God caused hail to fall on all of Egypt, destroying crops, trees, people and animals (Exod 9:22). Through this plague, God was showing power over the sky goddess Nut; it was her job to protect the people, livestock and crops from this kind of destruction, which she was unable to do.

It is clear that by the eighth plague, Pharaoh's heart, though still hardened, was having a more difficult time resisting the compelling case Moses was making for releasing Israel. Pharaoh even repented at this point, but then changed his mind again and kept Israel as slaves (Exod 9:27, 34). Moses then stretched out his hand over the land of Egypt, and the Lord caused a great wind which brought scores of locusts into the land to consume anything that the previous plagues had not destroyed (Exod 10:13). In this plague, Yahweh demonstrated His power over Senehem, the locust-headed god who was responsible for protecting the land from the ravages of pests.

In the ninth plague, Yahweh went after one of the most powerful gods in Egypt: the sun-god, Ra. He was chief among the gods of Egypt, and the other gods were often classified by their relation to him. Ra was the source of all life and growth. What did Moses do to defeat this god? At the command of Yahweh, he simply stretched out his hand toward heaven, and the land was overwhelmed with darkness for three days (Exod 10:22). This darkness was unlike any you or I have ever experienced; it was so dark that they could not see each other, and everyone stayed where they were sitting for the entirety of the three days.

In the next lesson, we will study the tenth plague and the release of Israel.

APPLICATION

Pharaoh's heart was hard as stone, no matter what form of discipline came upon him, he refused to repent and obey God. You can probably identify to some extent with this tendency. Are there any areas of your life in which God has been leading you to repentance, but you have been slow to respond? Taste and see that the Lord is good—He brings peace to those who turn to Him

ACTIVITIES

1. Draw It. Pick one of the first nine plagues and draw a picture on the following page of the destruction it might have caused in Egypt. Imagine the extent of the destruction that plague would have caused and attempt to capture it in your drawing.

- Waters to blood
- Frogs
- Lice
- Flies
- Livestock diseased
- Boils
- Hail
- Locusts
- Darkness

Lesson 5.2

Unit 5: The Exodus

2. Journal Time: A Soft Heart. Proverbs 28:14 (NIV) says: "Blessed is the man who always fears the LORD, but he who hardens his heart falls into trouble." Pharaoh is perhaps the clearest picture in the Bible of someone who hardened his heart. We are also capable of hardening our hearts like Pharaoh did. The harder our hearts get, the more difficult it is to see the hardness and soften them. Consider your own heart and answer the following questions in the space below.

- Pray and ask God to reveal any areas of your life where your heart is hard.
- Think through all the important relationships in your life: with your parents, siblings, teachers, mentors, and friends.

Are there any relationships that are suffering? _____
_____
_____
_____

Is there any hardness in your heart that could be causing the broken relationship? If so, confess this hardness to God and ask Him to soften your heart; write a short prayer of confession. _____
_____
_____
_____
_____

Is there any potential hardness in the heart of the other person that could be causing the broken relationship? If so, pray for them and write a short prayer of blessing. _____
_____
_____
_____

If the Lord reveals no hardness to you, don't count it out for sure, but be patient to see if God will reveal anything. Write a short prayer in praise to Him for keeping your heart soft. _____
_____
_____
_____

Lesson 5.2

EVALUATION

1. How did Pharaoh respond to Moses' initial request that he release Israel? _____
_____
_____

2. What did Israel think of Moses when their workload increased? _____
_____
_____

3. How did Moses respond to Israel's anger toward him for causing an increase in their workload? ___
_____
_____

4. What was the meaning of Aaron's serpent-rod consuming Pharaoh's magicians' serpent-rods? ___
_____
_____
_____
_____

5. Name three plagues and what Egyptian gods were defeated in them. _____
_____
_____
_____
_____

6. What was Pharaoh's general response to the plagues? _____
_____
_____

7. What was the state of Egypt after the first nine plagues? _____
_____
_____

LESSON 5.3

The Passover and Israel's Escape from Egypt

THE STORY

Lesson Theme - God crushed Pharaoh's head and delivered Israel.
The main point of this lesson is twofold. (1) God crushed Pharaoh's head by taking the Egyptians' firstborn sons *while* (2) He delivered Israel through their offering of a substitute lamb—a sacrifice which became their feast. Judgement and deliverance both cost blood. Both sides of the Passover story become paradigmatic images for judgement and deliverance throughout the Bible. God defeats His enemies by destroying the serpent's seed, and God delivers His people through a blood sacrifice which becomes a fellowship meal.

In the first nine plagues, God attacked various gods in the Egyptian pantheon. In this last plague, He went after Pharaoh himself. Pharaoh was considered a god in the Egyptian religion. At times, he was considered the incarnation of the god Horus, the son of Isis and Osiris. Other times, he was considered the son of Ra. Either way, the Egyptians viewed him as among the highest of the Egyptian gods. Of course, this last plague affected every family in Egypt, not only Pharaoh. Pharaoh, however, was the source of stability in the Egyptian culture; for Pharaoh to lose his son was a direct attack on his throne and deity. By killing his son, God was going after the seed of the serpent (Pharaoh being the serpent in this story). Throughout the Bible, we will see the seed of the woman defeating the serpent by defeating the serpent's seed.

OVERVIEW

The final plague that God brought on the Egyptians was the death of the firstborn. In order to be saved from the death of their own firstborns, the Israelites had to perform the Passover ceremony. That is, they had to select an unblemished lamb, kill it, put its blood on their doorposts and lintels, roast it and eat it that night. This ceremony became a ritual feast that Israel celebrated throughout their generations. In this way, God delivered Israel from the death of their firstborn sons and out of the land of Egypt.

SOURCE MATERIAL

- Exodus 11:1-13:22
- Psalm 77
- Proverbs 16:20
- *A Dictionary of Egyptian Gods and Goddesses* by George Hart

The previous nine plagues did not affect Israel or the areas where they were living. Repeatedly, the text tells us that God was making a distinction between Israel and Egypt. In this final plague, God continued to make a distinction between Israel and Egypt, but there was a difference from before. In the previous plagues, Israel didn't have to do anything in particular to protect themselves from the plague. In the tenth plague, however, they were told to follow very specific instructions in order to preserve themselves from the death of the firstborn.

Unit 5: The Exodus

OBJECTIVES

Feel...

- joy at God's victory in delivering Israel from Egypt.
- a sense of God's grace when He passed over the Israelites and preserved their firstborn sons.

Understand...

- that the death of the firstborn was a direct attack on Pharaoh.
- that Israel was not automatically exempt from the tenth plague as they had been from the other nine plagues.
- the requirements put on Israel to offer the Passover lamb in order to protect their firstborns.
- that the Passover was not just a one-time deliverance; the Passover feast became a central symbol of Israel's national identity.
- the significance of the blood on the doorposts.
- the significance of the Israelites eating the meat of the sacrifice.
- that although the foundation of the Israelites' deliverance was *faith* in the blood of the lamb, they still had to actually offer the lamb according to God's instructions in order to be delivered.

Apply this understanding by...

- identifying areas in your life where you are currently experiencing slavery.
- seeking God to determine what you are not believing about God that is preventing deliverance from these areas of slavery and what concrete steps you need to take to experience deliverance.

There are two aspects of Moses' instructions to Israel on how to prepare and perform the Passover. First, instructions were given on how to institute the Passover on the very night that the firstborns of Egypt would be killed. Second, instructions were given to them on the implementation of the annual Passover festival; even from the very beginning, God was preparing Israel to celebrate and recall what God did when He delivered them from Egypt.

What God was implementing in the Passover was incredibly important. The Passover was not a one-time event; it is one of the most important pictures in the Old Testament of how God interacts with His people. We too enjoy the benefits of this celebration in church today when we celebrate communion (also called the Lord's supper or the Eucharist). By implementing the Lord's supper on the day of the Passover meal, Jesus transformed the Passover: He showed that it had always been a picture of His death and resurrection.

For Israel in Egypt, to protect themselves from the death of their firstborns, each family had to (1) take one lamb without blemish on the 10th of the month, (2) kill it on the 14th of the month at twilight (this was the beginning of the day according to Hebrew reckoning), (3) take some of the blood and put it on the doorposts and lintel of their houses, (4) roast and eat the meat of the sacrificial lamb with bitter herbs and unleavened bread, and (5) eat the meal in haste, wearing their sandals and belt, so they would be ready to go when they were released (Exod 12:3-11).

There is a lot of symbolism in here, but to keep it simple, we'll focus on just a couple of points. First, the lamb was a substitute for the firstborn of the house; it was not as though Israel was somehow exempt from God's judgement. Israel was every bit as subject to God's judgement as Egypt was, but Israel was saved by their faith in the substitute. The blood was put on the doorposts and lintel of the house as a sign to the Lord that a substitute had died in place of the firstborn. This substitutionary sacrifice is an important theme in the Bible. Later, God would institute the sin offering for Israel where the lamb died for the sin of the worshiper; and of course, all of these sacrifices anticipated Jesus Christ's substitutionary sacrifice for us.

The second point of symbolism is the fact that the Israelites actually ate the meat of the sacrificial animal. Eating the sacrifice may seem odd at first, but it has loads of implications. That which had died for the people of Israel now sustained them, meaning that the Passover was not just a protection from judgement, but also a source of life. Furthermore, the Israelites were to share in the meal with their entire household; they were united by all eating the same meat from the same animal that died. The Passover is a *feast*, and feasts are times of celebration. Don't miss the fact that the Israelites ate a HUGE feast on this night. They were not allowed to save the meat and eat it the next week; they had to eat that whole animal, and if it was too much for them, they had to burn the leftovers the next morning (Exod 12:8, 10). God, in His grace, wanted them to eat way too much!

Notice the similarities between the Passover feast and communion. *We* eat the flesh and blood of our Lord when we partake of the elements. We eat the sacrificial meat as a life sustaining meal. When we eat that meal, we eat it in unity, because the same food sustains the life of all whom we partake with. Finally, symbolically, Jesus Himself becomes a part of each of us as we join in that meal.

In addition to instructions on how to perform the Passover that very night, Moses gave Israel instructions from God on how to celebrate the Passover as a feast year after year (Exod 12:14-20). First, this event was so significant that it recalibrated the calendar of Israel. The month in which Passover took place (Nissan) was to be the first month of their calendar from then on (Exod 12:2). In the future, the celebration of Passover would become a week-long festival. They would carefully remove all leaven from their houses and take all the days of that week as Sabbaths. Additionally, Moses instructed them that only those who had been circumcised could partake of the Passover; this feast was tied up with their national identity as Israel. Finally, because of God's protection of Israel's firstborn, from then on all firstborns were to be consecrated to the Lord as holy. These things were to be a reminder to Israel throughout their generations of how God had delivered them from Egypt and made them into a nation.

Israel's story is your story, and Israel is your people. If you attend a church where they perform communion, whether it is once a year, once a quarter, once a month or every week, you are partaking in a tradition that is rooted in Israel's exodus. God taught Moses to keep the Passover; Moses taught the people of Israel, who then taught their kids, who passed it down generation by generation, until Jesus learned it from His parents. Then He transformed Passover into communion and taught His disciples to keep it. When Peter preached the gospel on Pentecost, 5,000 people came to know the Lord in addition to the 120 who already knew Him. Every Christian today is a descendant of one of those people through evangelism. You are in a line of people who have kept this feast that goes all the way back to Moses. God has delivered you from sin and death with just as much power and glory as when He delivered Israel out of Egypt.

Israel performed the Passover and was delivered, while the Egyptians' firstborns died. In the middle of the night, Pharaoh summoned Moses and commanded him to take his people and leave (Exod 12:31). The people of Israel were all ready to go (that was how they were supposed eat the feast—all prepared to leave). As God had commanded the Israelites, they plundered their Egyptian neighbors by simply asking for valuables, for the Israelites had found favor in the eyes of the Egyptians (Exod 12:36). Moses took the bones of Joseph according to Joseph's request (Exod 13:19), and the Israelites took off.

APPLICATION

Slavery is a common condition of mankind. We all are bombarded with temptations that seek to take our identity, our calling and our relationship with God. The story of Israel's delivery from slavery in Egypt—the Passover story—provides us with a concrete image of how God always delivers His people from slavery.

First, to be delivered from slavery, we must believe that God is good and wants to save us. That is to say that salvation comes when we *trust* God. Proverbs 16:20 teaches that trusting God leads to happiness. Second, delivery requires that we *do* something. Israel would not have been delivered by simply trusting that God would pass over them; they had to kill the animal and paint their doors with it's blood.

What sort of slavery might you be under and what is God asking of you in order to find peace and deliverance?

ACTIVITIES

1. Family Tree: My Story. You are a part of the story of Moses and the people of Israel. If you have ever participated in a communion service (Lord's supper, Eucharist) you have participated in a practice that has been passed down generation after generation to this very day. Make a family tree style diagram on the following page (sort of like the seed-line diagram) with Moses at the top and your name at the bottom. From Moses' name, draw a short arrow down to "the people of Israel" then continue down to "Jesus and His disciples." Be creative in including intermediate "generations" all the way down to your name at the bottom.

Lesson 5.3

Unit 5: The Exodus

2. Journal Time: Belief and Action. We are all subject to different kinds of slavery, just like the Israelites were slaves to Pharaoh. When God delivered the Israelites from Egypt, He required that they have faith in Him and then act on that faith by offering the Passover lamb. God wants to deliver us from slavery as well and asks that we have faith in Him and act on that faith. Write about the following in the space below.

Spend some time in prayer, asking God to reveal an area in your life where you are a slave to some kind of sin. What did you hear from God? _____

_____
_____
_____
_____
_____

What does God want you to believe in order to overcome this area of slavery? _____

_____
_____
_____
_____
_____
_____
_____

What is God asking you to do to overcome this area of slavery? _____

_____
_____
_____
_____
_____

Lesson 5.3

EVALUATION

1. What Egyptian god was specifically addressed in the plague on the firstborn? _____

2. In the other nine plagues, Israel was automatically exempt; was this true in the plague on the firstborn? _____

3. Give a description of what the Israelites did the night of the death of the firstborn to protect their firstborn sons. _____

4. What was the significance of putting the blood on their doorposts? _____

5. What was the significance of eating the meat of the sacrifice? _____

6. What does the Passover have to do with *you*? _____

7. The Passover ritual became an annual feast; what all did the feast involve? _____

8. Who was allowed to participate in the annual Passover feast? _____

9. Why did Moses take the bones of Joseph when they fled from Egypt? _____

The Exodus From Egypt

Nuweiba Beach Crossing – Sinai at Jabal al-Lawz

Scale: 0 – 50 – 100 mi

Labeled locations:
- Egypt: Buto, Xois, Memphis, Heliopolis (On), Nile, Rameses, Goshen, Pithom, Succoth, Pelusium (Sin)
- Sinai / Red Sea area: Etham, Migdol, Pi Hahiroth, Red Sea, Gulf of Suez, Gulf of Aqaba, Ezion Geber
- Arabia / Midian: Elim, Marah, Wilderness of Sin, Rephidim (Meribah), Mt. Sinai, Wilderness of Shur, Midian
- Negev / Canaan: Kadesh Barnea, Hormah, Rehoboth, Zoar, Bozrah, Beersheba, Gaza, Gath, Hebron, Lod, Joppa, Shechem, Bethel, Jebus, Bethlehem, Jericho, Jazer, Heshbon, Dibon, Succoth, Mizpah
- Regions: Wilderness of Egypt, Wilderness of Paran, Wilderness of Zin, Amalek, Philistia, Edom, Moab, Ammon, Bashan, Canaan
- Waters: Great Sea, Brook of Egypt, Salt Sea, Sea of Galilee, Jordan, Jabbok, Arnon, Zered, Kishon

Annotation boxes:

- Israel traveled from Goshen by way of the Red Sea wilderness to Succoth (Exod 13:18-20).
- Israel camped before Pi Hahiroth between Israel and the Sea—they were trapped (Exod 14:2-3).
- Israel camped at a number of places before coming to Ezion Geber (Num 33:15-35).
- Israel traveled to Mara (Exod 15:22), then they camped near Elim (Exod 15:27), then on to Rephidim (Exod 17:1).
- Israel camped in the Wilderness of Sinai near Mt. Sinai (Exod 19:1-2).
- Israel came to Kadesh Barnea and wandered in the wilderness before heading north to conquer their enemies (Num 33:15-35).

LESSON 5.4

The Red Sea Crossing and the Song of Moses

UNIT 5

THE STORY

Lesson Theme - Israel baptized into life; Egypt baptized into death.

The Red Sea crossing was an act of God in which He baptized the Egyptians into death and baptized Israel into death and resurrection. God is a warrior, and He fought the battle for Israel. Notice in this story that Israel never brandished a sword or attacked a chariot; in fact, they went "under" the same water the Egyptians did! And yet the entire Egyptian army was defeated, while Israel was preserved. Rather, they were more than preserved; the Israelites were *baptized* into Moses (1 Cor 10:2). The crossing of the Red Sea was a defining moment for Israel. When they went into Egypt they were a family; while in Egypt, they became an oppressed people; after they passed through the Red Sea, they became a nation.

One of the key themes in this lesson is baptism and death. Water is a source of life—a truth found both in the real world and in the Bible (the Bible gives us the true way of interpreting the real world). Water brings life in two ways. First, water sustains life. Second, water brings resurrection life through death. When a person goes underwater, he dies; when God brings him out the other side, he is alive. He has been resurrected; he has been baptized. This is what baptism means when a believer goes through it, and this is what baptism meant for Israel when they went through the Red Sea. They came out on the other side with a more glorious kind of life.

OVERVIEW

God led Israel through the wilderness to the Red Sea where they were trapped with mountains all around, the sea before them, and the Egyptian army in pursuit. Afraid they were going to die, the Israelites complained against the Lord and Moses, but Moses encouraged them to trust in the Lord. Then God miraculously opened the sea and led the Israelites through a death and resurrection experience in the sea (a baptism of sorts). The Egyptian armies pursued them into the sea and were drowned in the water. Israel responded well and praised the Lord for delivering them.

SOURCE MATERIAL

- Exodus 14-15
- Psalm 20
- Proverbs 20:24
- *The Red Sea Rules* by Robert Morgan

This lessons provides some incredibly potent practical lessons about how to face hardship. Spend some time driving these lessons home. For the content of these practical lessons, we are drawing on a book called "The Red Sea Rules" by Robert Morgan. We encourage purchasing a copy of this book to get an in-depth look at these lessons. The Red Sea rules according to Morgan are as follows:

1. <u>Realize that God means for you to be where you are.</u> God had planned Israel's history,

Unit 5: The Exodus

OBJECTIVES

Feel...

- the hopelessness that Israel felt being surrounded by mountains, the Red Sea and Pharaoh's armies.
- anticipation of how God would deliver the nation.
- the joy of Israel's celebration on the far side of the Red Sea.

Understand...

- that the crossing of the Red Sea was a kind of baptism (death and resurrection) for Israel.
- that baptism is a way of life in God's world; He gives life *through* death.
- practical things to do when facing a trial (the Red Sea rules).
- the importance of celebrating when God does something good in your life.

Apply this understanding by...

- evaluating how you have behaved during trials in your own life.
- implementing the Red Sea rules to any current trials you may have.
- celebrating your own deliverance by singing Exodus 15.

and it was working out according to His plan. Exodus 13:18 says that "God led the people around by way of the wilderness of the Red Sea." When they got there, they were trapped by the sea on their east, the armies of Pharaoh on the west and mountains all around; yet, all of this was ordained by God.

2. <u>Be more concerned for God's glory than your relief.</u> In Exodus 14:4 God says, "I will gain honor over Pharaoh and over all his army." God's purpose in trapping Israel was to bring glory to Himself *through Israel's deliverance*. Their deliverance was not a separate issue; but nonetheless, God was interested in His glory *first*. In our trials, God wants us to seek His deliverance for the sake of His glory, not for the sake of deliverance in itself.

3. <u>Acknowledge your enemy, but keep your eyes on the Lord.</u> Israel provides us with a negative example here; they told Moses, "Because there were no graves in Egypt, have you taken us away to die in the wilderness? Why have you so dealt with us, to bring us up out of Egypt?" (Exod 14:11). But Moses encouraged them to look to the Lord (Exod 14:13-14).

4. <u>Pray.</u> Israel did cry out to the Lord (Exod 14:10), but their cry was followed by complaint, for they were operating out of fear. Moses gives us an example of calm trust in the Lord.

5. <u>Stay calm and confident, and give God time to work.</u> We often want God to rush to our aid, but He often waits for us to look to Him with trust. Moses' response to Israel's complaints exemplifies the kind of trust we should have in the Lord: "Do not be afraid. Stand still, and see the salvation of the LORD, which He will accomplish for you today. For the Egyptians whom you see today, you shall see again no more forever. The LORD will fight for you, and you shall hold your peace" (Exod 14:13-14).

6. <u>When unsure, just take the next logical step by faith.</u> God told Israel to start moving toward the Red Sea *before* He had parted it: "Why do you cry to Me? Tell the children

Unit 5: The Exodus

of Israel to go forward. But lift up your rod, and stretch out your hand over the sea and divide it. And the children of Israel shall go on dry ground through the midst of the sea" (Exod 15:15-16). Sometimes God calls us to walk in a direction that makes no sense and even appears as though it will lead to death; trust Him and walk where He leads. "A man's steps are of the LORD; how then can a man understand his own way?" (Prov 20:24).

7. <u>Envision God's enveloping presence.</u> This was easier for Israel than it often is for us. While they could see the pillar of cloud before them (Exod 14:19-20), we walk by faith. Go where God leads even when you can't see Him; believe He is really there, because *He is*.

8. <u>Trust God to deliver in His own unique way.</u> Often God delivers miraculously *through* a death-like experience. For Israel, this meant that God caused the wind to blow to part the sea (Exod 14:21). You will probably not be able to foresee *how* God will deliver you, but trust Him anyway. Walking with God gets exciting when we learn to trust Him even when we cannot see.

9. <u>View your current crisis as a faith builder for the future.</u> God is not that interested in simply solving your problems; He is trying to test your faith and grow you into maturity. After God had delivered Israel, they were a changed people; they "feared the LORD, and believed the LORD and His servant Moses" (Exod 14:31).

10. <u>Don't forget to praise Him.</u> After Israel had gone through their baptism and experienced their death and resurrection, they sang a song to the Lord (Exod 15).

Go back and read through the underlined portion of the 10 rules and ask God to reveal which is most relevant to your life. Spend some time meditating, seeking the Lord and repenting to God in any area of life God is calling you to.

ACTIVITIES

1. Journal Time.

Think of the last time you faced a difficult hardship in life and consider the questions below.

Describe the trial._____

_____

_____

_____

_____

_____

_____

Lesson 5.4

How did you respond? _____

_____

_____

_____

_____

_____

What should you have done differently? _____

_____

_____

_____

In what ways did you respond properly?_____

_____

_____

_____

If you are currently facing a trial, write down some practical steps you can take to implement the lessons of Israel at the Red Sea (see the Red Sea rules)._____

_____

_____

_____

_____

2. Sing: "The Song of Moses and the Song of the Lamb." This story is your story. In Revelation 15:2-3 it says that the inhabitants of heaven (that's us!) will sing the song of Moses and the song of the Lamb. The song of the Lamb is in Revelation 15:3-4; the song of Moses is recorded in Exodus 15. Exodus 15:1, 20-21 indicate that a portion of the song was sung by the men, with the women answering responsively with tambourines. This song has been structured to try to capture that; guys and ladies parts are indicated in the words on the following page.

The Song of Moses and the Song of the Lamb
Melody: HEAR THE CALL OF THE KINGDOM by Keith Getty and Stuart Townsend
Words: Adapted by Joe Anderson

Song of Moses:
(guys only)
I will sing out to Yahweh
He has gained victory
For the horse and its rider
He has thrown into the sea
He's my song and my power
He has saved me from death
I exalt and praise my father's God

(everyone)
Call Him Yahweh, He is mighty in war
Pharaoh's armies have been thrown in the sea
And his captains have been drowned like a stone
Yahweh is our God, our God alone

(guys only)
In Your right hand is power
It has crushed all our foes
In Your great wrath and glory
You consumed those You oppose
They were set on destruction
When You blew with Your wind
And the walls of water covered them

Our God Yahweh, who has glory like You
You are holy, and You're fearful in praise
By Your right hand Egypt drowned in the grave
But Your people have all been saved

(guys only)
Now the nations of Canaan
Where Your people will dwell
Will hear tell of Your power
And how Egypt surely fell

When they're frozen with terror
At the greatness of God
We'll march through them to Your holy hill

(everyone)
He is Yahweh, He will give us a home
In His mountain, He prepared long ago
He will plant us in His sanctuary
Yahweh is our God eternally

(ladies only, with tambourines)
Sing to Yahweh, He has gained victory
Horse and rider, He has thrown in the sea,
Sing to Yahweh, He has gained victory
He has triumphed o'er the enemy

Song of the Lamb: *(everyone)*
Your works are great and mighty
Just and true are Your ways
You're the Lord God Almighty
And the King of all the saints
All the nations will fear You
And Your name glorify
For Your judgments have been proven right.

He is Yahweh, He will give us a home
In His mountain, He prepared long ago
He will plant us in His sanctuary
Yahweh is our God eternally

Lesson 5.4

EVALUATION

1. In what way was Israel's crossing the Red Sea a "baptism"? _____
_____
_____
_____
_____

2. Name the ten Red Sea rules. _____
_____
_____
_____
_____
_____
_____
_____
_____
_____
_____

3. What did Israel do after they had crossed the Red Sea? _____
_____
_____

LESSON 5.5

Israel Developed a Habit of Complaint; God Continued to Provide

THE STORY

Lesson Theme - Trusting God's patience
This lesson is about two things. First: don't complain; God doesn't like it! Second: trust God's character, particularly His kindness and patience. It will be very easy for you to allow the first point to overshadow the second, and that would be a serious mistake. You *must* see that God's heart for Israel—and for you—is for good. *That* is what makes it possible to trust God enough to lament instead of complaining.

The story
After being delivered from Pharaoh's army, Israel followed Moses three days' journey into the desert, where they ran out of water. Finally they found some water, but it was bitter. In this context, "bitter" doesn't just mean that it tasted bad; they would have been happy to drink bad-tasting water at this point. "Bitter" means the water was polluted, probably alkaline, to the point of being undrinkable. They named the place "Marah" which means "bitter" and complained to Moses (Exod 15:22-24).

Moses prayed, and God showed him a tree to put into the water. When he did, the water miraculously turned sweet (Exod 15:25). At this point, God also gave the Israelites a gentle warning: "If you diligently heed the voice of the LORD your God and do what is right in His sight, give ear to His commandments and keep all His statutes, I will put none of the diseases on you which I have brought on the Egyptians. For I am the LORD who heals you" (Exod 15:26). Israel had complained against Yahweh repeatedly ever

OVERVIEW

Israel had crossed the Red Sea and was now following the Lord through the wilderness, but they had not learned to trust God and were continuing their nasty habit of complaining. They complained in Egypt, they complained to the Lord before they crossed the Red Sea, and it seems as though no amount of miraculous deliverance could teach them to trust the Lord. In this lesson, we see how Israel failed to trust the Lord in two different ways. First, they failed to trust the Lord for food and complained against the Lord and Moses, and God provided them with a steady stream of manna from heaven. Second, they failed to trust the Lord for water and complained again, and God provided water from a rock. After this, God showed again that He was on Israel's side and would fight their battles for them by defeating the Amalekites. The point of this lesson is twofold. First, God is a merciful Provider; His heart for us is for good even when we are not faithful. Second, He is a good Father who knows that we need to grow into mature obedience—but He won't tolerate immaturity forever. He does eventually require mature obedience from us.

SOURCE MATERIAL

- Exodus 15:22-17:16
- Psalms 13, 95
- Proverbs 11:28
- Hebrews 3:7-4:13

Unit 5: The Exodus

OBJECTIVES

Feel...

- surprise that Israel would so quickly forget how good God had been to them.
- shock at the intense nature of Israel's complaining.
- concern that you might complain too much.
- initial puzzlement that complaining is forbidden, but lament is encouraged.
- trust that God is not seeking to punish His people, but to grow them.

Understand...

- that God waited to insist on obedience until He had established a track record of goodness toward Israel.
- that God allows people to grow into His requirements for mature obedience; He doesn't require mature obedience all at once.
- that the third cycle of complaint (at Massah and Meribah) was the beginning of the end for the exodus generation.
- that lament is honestly laying the problem before God and asking Him to intervene.
- that complaint is telling God He messed up.

Apply this understanding by...

- identifying an area in your life where God is slowly increasing His requirements for mature obedience and trust and stepping up to the challenge.

since Moses had arrived in Egypt, but up to this point, Yahweh had always just reassured the Israelites that He would do what He said. Now Yahweh warned them that they needed to listen to Him and keep His laws. They now had enough history with Yahweh to know that He intended good for them.

As the Israelites continued to travel, God brought them to Elim, where there were twelve wells of water. After camping at Elim, God then led them to the Wilderness of Sin, where they began to run short on food. Again, Israel complained against Moses and Aaron, and the complaints got sharper (Exod 16:3). Yahweh responded that He would rain bread from heaven, but that it would also be a test to see whether Israel would keep His laws or not. He instructed Moses and Aaron to tell the people to gather only enough food for one day, except on Friday, when they should gather and prepare twice as much food so they wouldn't work on the Sabbath. Then when Moses and Aaron gathered the people, God's glory appeared in a cloud that came down to the ground, and God spoke to Moses in front of the whole nation and told them that they would have meat in the evening and bread in the morning, so that they would know He was God (Exod 16:4-12).

In the evening, as God had said, quail came into the camp; and in the morning, there was something on the ground after the dew lifted. The people asked Moses what it was, and he told them it was the bread God was giving them (Exod 16:15). Then Moses instructed them to gather only what they needed for that day. Moses explicitly told them to eat all they had gathered and leave none until morning, but some of the people saved it overnight. God made sure to expose their disobedience, because it turned out this stuff didn't keep overnight. In the morning,

Lesson 5.5

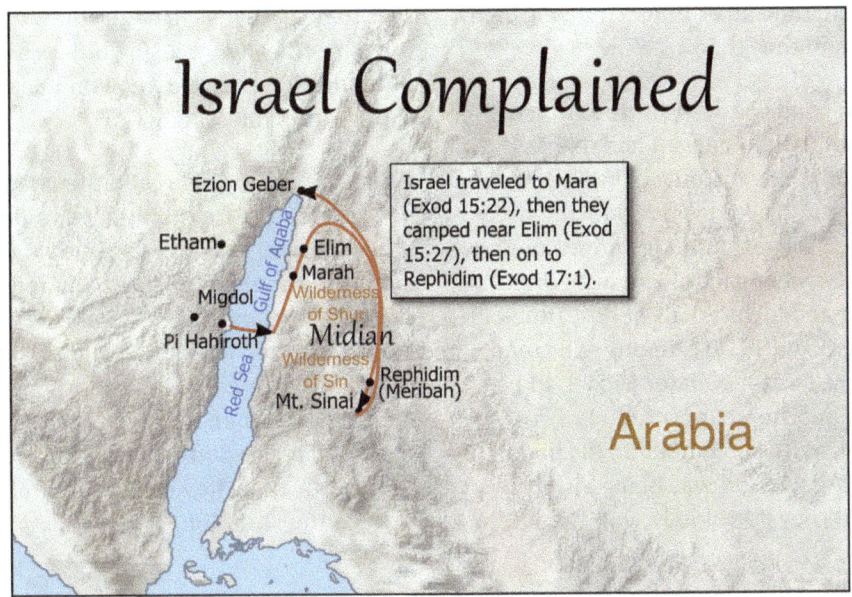

the bread was full of worms, and it stank (Exod 16:20). That was a relatively gentle reminder that God's way really was the best way, and bad things would happen if they didn't obey. Israel did not heed this warning, and ultimately, their disobedience would kill them.

On Friday, Moses told the people to gather twice as much bread and prepare it ahead of time, and it would keep until morning (Exod 16:22-23). They followed Moses' instructions, and the bread kept for the Sabbath. Moses told them to eat and rest on the Sabbath. Some of the people went out into the fields to gather anyway—but there wasn't anything to gather. Then the Lord rebuked them for refusing to listen to His commandments (Exod 16:28-29).

The Israelites called the bread from heaven "manna," which literally means "What is it?" (Exod 16:15, 31). God commanded them to save a bowl of manna so they would remember what they had eaten in the wilderness. The manna continued to fall six days a week for the entire time they were in the wilderness until they came to Canaan (Exod 16:32-36).

Then the Lord led Israel away from the Wilderness of Sin and brought them to Rephidim, where once again, there was no water (Exod 17:1). The people again complained that Moses and Aaron were going to kill them with thirst. Moses cried out to God, and God told Moses to stand on "the rock in Horeb," which appears to have been some kind of recognizable geological feature (Exod 17:6). God told him to strike the rock with the staff he had used to strike the Nile. Moses did, and water flowed. Then Moses named the place Massah ("testing") and Meribah ("rebellion") because the people tested God by accusing Him of being unwilling to care for them (Exod 17:7). Notice that even though the people had *this specific problem* before, as soon as it happened again, they started accusing God

Unit 5: The Exodus

of trying to kill them. The people were just not learning from their mistakes here. God was being good to them, and they didn't see it.

Following the second water crisis, the Amalekites came down to fight against Israel (Exod 17:8). After sending Joshua out with the warriors to fight, Moses stood on a hill overlooking the battle. And when Moses raised his hands over the battlefield, Israel began to win, but when Moses got tired and lowered his hands, Amalek started winning (Exod 17:11). Seeing the trend, Aaron and Hur put a stone under Moses so he could sit down, and they supported his arms from either side so he could hold up his hands until sundown. Again, God was being visibly good to Israel. If they had simply won the battle, they might have been able to tell themselves that they were just stronger than the Amalekites. But since they were losing unless Moses held his hands up, they clearly won because of God's supernatural blessing.

Notice also that God made the Israelites actually fight the battle. He didn't have to do that—many times in Israel's history God would vanquish the enemy without Israel doing anything at all. God could have bombed the Amalekites with hailstones, opened a sinkhole and swallowed up the whole army, or confused them so that they attacked each other. He didn't. Instead, He allowed the Israelites to do the work themselves, but in such a way that they were cooperating with His work in the situation.

APPLICATION

We often let ourselves believe that if we follow God's instructions, we should have no difficulties. That's just not the case, as Israel's story shows us here. God led them into places where there was no water and no food, then fed them with bread from the sky. God later interprets these events in Deuteronomy 8:3-5. In a nutshell, God allowed Israel to experience hardship so that they would know how much they really needed Him. In the same way, if we follow God, He will lead us into places of difficulty and need. The Good Shepherd takes us to green pastures and still waters, but also into the valley of the shadow of death.

ACTIVITIES

1. Complaint *versus* Lament. Read and examine Israel's complaints from Exodus 15 through 17 and compare to David's lament in Psalm 13. Write a paragraph below explaining the differences between the two. Explain why lament is good and complaint is bad. _____

_____

_____

_____

_____

2. Journal Time: Slow Teaching. God slowly built a foundation of kindness toward Israel so they would learn to trust Him. Then, God began to call them to trust Him in the way that they should. Identify one area in your own life where God is increasing His requirement for mature obedience and trust. Consider the following questions as you write a response in the space below.

What could you have gotten away with a few years ago that you can't now?_____
_____
_____
_____
_____
_____
_____

What do your younger siblings get away with that you can't?_____
_____
_____
_____
_____
_____
_____
_____

What do you have to do now that you didn't have to do this time last year?_____
_____
_____
_____
_____
_____
_____

Unit 5: The Exodus

Is there something hard you did this year that you couldn't have done before? _____
_____
_____
_____
_____
_____
_____

Is there something hard that God is asking you to do right now? _____
_____
_____
_____
_____
_____
_____
_____

Lesson 5.5

EVALUATION

1. How long did it take after Israel's celebration by the Red Sea for them to start complaining? _____

2. What was their first complaint? _____

3. What was their second complaint? _____

4. How did God resolve these complaints? _____
_____

5. How did God test their obedience the second time? _____
_____

6. What was the third complaint? _____

7. How did God resolve it? _____

8. How did God go about calling Israel to trust Him? _____
_____
_____

LESSON 5.6

Israel Distanced Herself from God and His Prophet

UNIT 5

THE STORY

Lesson Theme - Israel lost their chance for a close relationship with Moses and with God.

In the previous lesson, we learned how Israel complained, and God provided for them. God was proving His goodness to Israel before insisting on obedience from them. In this lesson, God gave Israel the opportunity to have a close relationship with Moses as God's prophet and with God Himself, but they squandered both of these opportunities out of sin.

This passage begins with Jethro, Moses' father-in-law, coming to bring Moses' wife and children back to him. After hearing of all that God had done for Israel, Jethro believed in God. Note especially Exodus 18:11—Jethro knew the Egyptian pantheon and saw the plagues upon Egypt in that light. Yahweh humbled the gods of the Egyptians, and hallowed (set apart) His name through the events of the exodus. Jethro worshiped the God of Israel as a result (Exod 18:12).

Israel had so many quarrels with one another that they kept Moses busy from morning until night every day, settling disputes (Exod 18:13-18). The burden was so great that one man couldn't bear it; Jethro gave Moses excellent advice, which Moses took: to set up a small bureaucracy of judges working under Moses who would settle petty disputes so Moses would only have to handle the really hard ones (Exod 18:19-23). Implementing a bureaucracy would never have been necessary if Israel could have resolved their own disputes by walking with God themselves. Because they overburdened Moses

OVERVIEW

Israel had the opportunity to have a close relationship with Moses, God's prophet, but they missed that opportunity by generating so many conflicts that Moses couldn't handle them all. Moses was forced to institute a bureaucracy just to avoid exhaustion. Israel then repeated the mistake with God. He gave Israel the opportunity to have a direct relationship with Him as His nation of priests, but because Israel did not trust God's covenant, they missed that opportunity as well, and so Moses became the intermediary who gave Israel God's revelation.

SOURCE MATERIAL

- Exodus 18-20:21
- Psalm 107
- Proverbs 1:8-9
- James 4:1, 8-10

the prophet, they were now separated from the prophet by a bureaucracy—a capable bureaucracy filled with honorable men, to be sure, but a separation nonetheless. It was Israel's sin that created the need for such a distance (see Jas 4:1).

This passage records three separate exchanges with God at Sinai. The first exchange established the nature and boundaries of God's relationship with Israel (Exod 19:1-15). God used Moses as His intermediary to propose the covenant to Israel, and Israel agreed to it. (This is an important

Unit 5: The Exodus

OBJECTIVES

Feel...

- amazement that Israel would refuse the relationship with God that He offered them.
- awe at God's majesty as He descended to the mountain.
- gratitude that we have the relationship with God that Israel avoided.

Understand...

- that Israel's sins generated so many quarrels that Moses could only resolve them all by working all day, every day.
- that Israel's quarrels arose from their consistent sin. Therefore, it was Israel's sin that required a large bureaucracy of intermediaries between the people and Moses as God's prophet.
- that Jethro's counsel was wisdom from God even though he was a new believer.
- that the people had an opportunity for a kind of face-to-face relationship with God at Sinai.
- that the people gave up the opportunity to have a face-to-face relationship with God by asking Moses to mediate between them and God.

Apply this understanding by...

- praising God for His goodness in providing us with direct relationship with Him.
- considering how your sin might create distance between you and God or between you and God's representatives.
- considering whether there are areas in your life where you might prefer rules over relationship with God.

---

pattern: first the covenant and *then* the intimacy; not the other way around. Sexual intimacy works the same way.)

The established covenant set up boundaries within which intimacy could take place. To that end, God then had His second exchange with Moses (Exod 19:16-25), where He reminded Israel of the terms within which they could have an intimate encounter with Him. He did not want to begin the relationship by killing a careless Israelite who wandered across the boundary. He sent Moses back down the mountain to underscore the seriousness of the point. (Throughout the Old Testament, this would be the way people came near to God: they were invited to come near, but not *too* near.)

Then, while Moses was at the foot of the mountain once again, warning Israel not to come up the mountain, God initiated the third exchange by speaking audibly to all the people (Exod 20:1-21). Since the people had already agreed to His covenant, they should have known that God wasn't going to kill them by speaking to them from the mountain. The covenant promised to protect them. But the people didn't trust God's good intentions for them and didn't remember the terms of the covenant that God had just agreed to (Exod 20:18).

Because of their fear, the people insisted (unnecessarily) on an intermediary (Exod 20:19-21). So the rest of the revelation given from the mountain (the vision of the tabernacle, the feasts, and so on) was given only to Moses instead of to all Israel directly.

We'll come back to this in another lesson, but here is something to think about: all that additional revelation took time, time during which Israel grew restive waiting for Moses at the bottom of the mountain and had their dalliance with the golden calf. If they had been willing to enter into the relationship God was offering, they would all have heard God's revelation from the mountain; for 40 days they would all have been taught by God, and the golden calf incident would never have happened. The whole history of Israel would have been different.

APPLICATION

Psalm 107 expresses the psalmist's desire for men to be grateful to God for what He has done. It was exactly in this area that Israel failed at Sinai. Instead of thanking God for the opportunity He was giving them and the covenant protection He had offered, they drew away from Him in terror. Avoid making the same mistake in their own lives by praising the Lord through this psalm.

ACTIVITIES

1. Make a List. List all the times since God sent Moses to Egypt that the Israelites were afraid God was going to kill them. Then make a corresponding list of reasons why the Israelites should not have been afraid, based on what God had revealed to them and done for them up to that point. Use the space below to make your lists.

The times the Israelites were afraid	Why they should not have been afraid

Unit 5: The Exodus

2. Sinai Timeline. Carefully read Exodus 18-20 and develop a timeline of events at Mt. Sinai. Exactly what happened, and in what order? Mark the events on the vertical line below. Earliest at the top and latest at the bottom.

Lesson 5.6

EVALUATION

1. Who was Jethro? Why was he coming to Moses? _____
_____

   Why might Moses not have wanted his wife and children with him in Egypt? _____
_____

2. Why did Moses listen to Jethro's advice? _____
_____

3. Why did Moses need to appoint so many leaders? _____
_____

4. What was the result of Moses appointing all those leaders? _____
_____
_____

5. Describe the sequence of events at Mt. Sinai. _____
_____
_____
_____
_____
_____

6. Why does the sequence of events matter? _____
_____
_____

7. Why did Israel squander their opportunity? _____
_____
_____
_____

LESSON 5.7

Moses Met with God and Received the Law

THE STORY

Lesson Theme - Keeping the character of the Law
In the previous lesson, we looked at how Israel dodged a direct relationship with God by getting Moses to be their intermediary. Right before that happened, God spoke directly to the whole nation from the top of the mountain and gave them the Ten Commandments. The Ten Commandments are far more than just a set of ten rules. They are a call to become a certain kind of person and to live in relationship with God in order to make that possible.

If you want to pile up the whole Old Testament Law under a couple of really big headings, it goes like this: all the Law and the Prophets hang on the two greatest commandments: love God with everything you've got, and love your neighbor as yourself (Matt 22:37-40). If you want a few more headings—and therefore a little more specific direction—you can turn to the Ten Commandments.

This lesson will focus on the Ten Commandments, although after Israel rejected His overtures, God also delivered several chapters of additional laws. As you look at that additional material, you'll see that it fits under the headings we find in the Ten Commandments (see the "Sorting the Law" activity).

In the Sermon on the Mount, Jesus showed how to read the Ten Commandments. In His treatment of the sixth and seventh commandments, He showed that it's not enough simply to keep the letter of the Law; God's people must have the character that the Law indicates (Matt 5:21-28). (See the discussion of the sixth and seventh commandments.) The same thing is true for the other eight commandments, as we will see.

Don't skip over Exodus 20:1-2 in a rush to get to the Ten Commandments. These verses show us that even while God was preparing to give the Law, He began with relationship: Who He was and how He related to the people who were listening to Him. He gave them their place in the Story: they had been rescued from Egypt by God.

OVERVIEW

Having made a covenant with Israel to give them the security of His promises, God then spoke directly to Israel, giving ten specific commands designed to guide the Israelites into loving God and their neighbors. When Israel recoiled in fear from direct relationship with God, He then began to elaborate on His commands, giving them what they wanted: law in place of relationship. But God still sought relationship with the people of Israel through the commands that He gave them.

SOURCE MATERIAL

- Exodus 20-24, especially 20:1-17
- Psalm 19
- Proverbs 3:1-2
- 1 Timothy 1:5-11
- R. J. Rushdoony, *The Institutes of Biblical Law*

Unit 5: The Exodus

OBJECTIVES

Feel...

- inadequacy in the face of the demands of the Law.

Understand...

- that the requirements of the Law were not arbitrary; they reflect the character of God.
- that the more detailed demands of the Law all fit under the headings of the Ten Commandments.
- that each of the Ten Commandments is an umbrella that encompasses a whole range of behavior and character.

Apply this understanding by...

- exploring how the details of the Law fit under the general headings of the Ten Commandments.
- considering how your own conduct measures up against the demands of the Law.
- learning to be a God-honoring person by seeking the center of God's commands, not seeing how close you can get to the edge of God's commands without breaking them.

Only then, from that foundation of grace, did God begin to give the Law.

The first four commandments relate to God; the last six to one's neighbor.

1. You shall have no other gods before Me (Exod 20:3). On the surface and at its most basic, this is a command against idolatry, and it flows directly from Exodus 20:1-2. Remember Jethro's comment in Exodus 18:11, "Now I know that the LORD is greater than all the gods." Also remember that it was Yahweh, not any of the Canaanite gods Israel still worshiped (see Amos 5:25-27, Acts 7:42-43) Who delivered them. He rescued them where no other god could; He required worship commensurate with what He had done for them.

2. You shall not make for yourself a carved image—any likeness of anything that is in heaven above, or that is in the earth beneath, or that is in the water under the earth; you shall not bow down to them nor serve them (Exod 20:4-5). At first glance, the second commandment seems a repetition of the first, but it only seems that way to us *because* we are so used to the idea that God may not be worshiped by bowing down to a statue. What we fail to understand is that among all the cultures around Israel, universally, the gods were worshiped through images. In that environment, the point of the second command was to forbid a certain *mode* of worship, a certain liturgical habit. Israel, as Yahweh's own special people (Exod 19:5), was never to worship images. No god—not even Yahweh—could be worshiped in this way in Israel, ever. Aaron violated this command almost immediately by making a golden calf, and Jeroboam would later violate this same command by instituting worship in two false temples with golden calves (1Kgs 12:25-33). This command has sometimes been taken to forbid making images of any sort at all, which is clearly not the case (see Exod 25:33, 26:1, 1 Kgs 7).

Notice also that the second commandment came with an explanatory statement (Exod 20:5-6) that specifically promised God would pursue judgment on this sin through the generations until the people repented. Some folks have made much of this sort of generational sin, but all a person need do to escape God's judgment is to love God and keep His commandments, which is the point of Exodus 20:6.

3. You shall not take the name of the LORD your God in vain (Exod 20:7). In contemporary Christian culture, this commandment is generally taken as a prohibition of swearing ("Oh God!" and the like). While this is a legitimate application of the command, it goes a lot further than that. Invoking God's authority for something He didn't say, whether it's a false teaching, a false prophecy, or a legalistic standard of righteousness, violates this command (in Jesus' words, "Teaching as doctrines the commandments of men" [Matt 15:9]).

4. Remember the Sabbath day, to keep it holy (Exod 20:8). Notice that this command extends to servants and visiting foreigners (Exod 20:10). God would later ask for one tenth of Israel's money as an offering; but first of all, He asked for one seventh of their time. The Sabbath was a blessed and holy feast day, a day set aside for celebration, worship, and rest; and therefore, no work was to be done on it. There's a too-common tendency to focus on what Israel was *not* allowed to do on the Sabbath, which misses the point. The focus should be on what Israel was supposed *to do* on the Sabbath: rest and experience God's blessing. (See also Lev 26 for further discussion of the Sabbath as a feast day.) We'll focus on feasts in a later lesson, so we recommend you pass over this command lightly.

The fourth commandment is also a theological landmine because Christians have differing convictions on whether Sabbath observance is a continuing requirement today. For the purposes of this lesson, modern-day Sabbath observance is a rathole we recommend you not crawl into; suffice it to say that it was certainly required of Israel, and we are directly forbidden to fight about it (Rom 14:5-10).

5. Honor your father and your mother (Exod 20:12). Notice that the fifth commandment is a positive command. There's no end to the possible ways to honor someone. It's not the sort of command you can ever say, "Okay, I've checked off the box, and I'm done with that;" there's always more. If you're a box-checker, this is bad news. But if you want to grow into loving like God does, the good news is you'll never exhaust His heart for you. Notice also that this command comes with a promise of long life. Proverbs 3:1-2 reflects on this promise.

6. You shall not murder (Exod 20:13). This is a prohibition, which makes box-checkers happy. Just don't kill anyone, and you can be sure you've kept the command, right? Not so fast. The prohibitions exist because of something positive that God values—in this case, life itself. If your goal is to hear God's heart in the command and follow Him rather than to simply check off a box and say, "I have kept the command," then commands like Deuteronomy 22:8 also come naturally; and the extension to animal control (Exod 21:28-32) is obvious. Jesus' own commentary on this command included hating your neighbor without cause in your heart (Matt 5:21-22). If our goal is not just to regulate our outward behavior but to have God's heart, Jesus' application is obvious: murder begins with hatred, and if you would be a life-giver in all ways rather than a life-taker, you must love people rather than hate them.

7. You shall not commit adultery (Exod 20:14). The seventh commandment requires marital faithfulness. Jesus again extended this command to the imagination and the heart (Matt 5:27-28).

8. You shall not steal (Exod 20:15). God has property rights; as His image, human beings also have property rights. Negatively, as stated, this means you don't take things that don't belong to you—money, things, property, reputation, and so on. (Gossip, for example, violates this command by taking another person's reputation.) As the Law would later extend it positively, the command includes actively protecting your neighbor's property (e.g., Exod 23:4), even if he doesn't like you.

9. You shall not bear false witness against your neighbor (Exod 20:16). This command is often quoted as "You shall not lie" which is a slightly broader way of stating the same principle: a devotion to truth. The more specific expression in the Ten Commandments puts the direct focus on courtroom proceedings—don't perjure yourself in order to gain some advantage against your neighbor.

10. You shall not covet your neighbor's house; you shall not covet your neighbor's wife, nor his male servant, nor his female servant, nor his ox, nor his donkey, nor anything that is your neighbor's (Exod 20:17). Notice the comprehensiveness of this command and the fact that this command is explicitly directed toward the heart. The positive side to this command is being content with what God has given. A lack of contentment issues in lust after the things God has given to other people, which is a violation of this command.

The tenth commandment is a good demonstration of how the commands are all interrelated. Protecting your neighbor's property (eighth commandment) is difficult if you lust after his property; remaining faithful to your own spouse (seventh commandment) is difficult if you lust after your neighbor's; greed makes it difficult to care for your parents properly as they get older (fifth commandment), while contentment makes it easier; and so on. Paul links the tenth commandment back to the first in Colossians 3:5, saying, "Put to death...covetousness, which is idolatry." When we say, "If only I had *that*, I would be happy," we are making *that* our god and putting another god before Yahweh.

Notice that because Israel had failed to trust God's good heart for them (see previous lesson), now God invited only Moses and some representatives up on the mountain. They saw God (Exod 24:10), but Israel did not. Then God called Moses, alone, up into the thick darkness for 40 days.

APPLICATION

There are two ways to respond to God's commands. We can look for the edges, or we can look for the center. If we look for the edges of the command, we find ourselves always trying to gratify our lusts by means that are *technically* legal. Adultery is off-limits, of course, but if a man's just *looking*...technically he's okay, right? Jesus said no; looking at a woman lustfully is also off-limits. Suppose the man says, "Well, all right, but suppose I'm not looking at an actual woman, just a picture of one?" That's okay, right? Nope; it's still a real woman who belongs to someone else, not to him. But the man who's looking for the edge of the command is not satisfied. "Suppose what I'm looking at is a *drawing* of a *totally imaginary* woman—Wonder Woman, Daphne from Scooby Doo, or Jean Grey from X-Men? She's not even real, so she can't belong to someone else—so that's totally okay, right?" Well...no.

The man is trying to cover himself legally by finding the edge of the law, but the root problem here is that the man is trying to please himself. He is missing the whole point. The point is relationship with God—to become the sort of person who relates effectively to God. To become that sort of person, we don't look for the edge of the law, but the center. By forbidding adultery, what sort of person is God seeking? He is seeking the sort of wives who are faithful to their husbands and the sort of husbands who are faithful to their wives. A man who is seeking to be faithful to his wife does not look for legal ways to lust for other women—he looks for ways to be enamored with the woman God has given him.

The same applies to all of the Ten Commandments. God's commands are for our good. If we seek to become the sort of person the command calls for, we will relate to God better and have better lives ourselves. So we should seek to be the sort of people who love God, worship Him alone and don't invoke His name lightly, rest well, honor our parents, forgive one another, grow in marital faithfulness, respect other people's property, speak the truth, and remain content with what God has given to us.

ACTIVITIES

1. Sorting the Law. In this lesson, we spent a lot of time on the Ten Commandments. The remainder of the Law is an elaboration on the basic principles laid out in the Ten Commandments. Read through Exodus 20:22-21:36 and identify which of the Ten Commandments (listed below) applies in each law within the passage. In the table on the next page, write which of the Ten Commandments is most relevant to the passage on the left.

1. You shall have no other gods before Me (Exod 20:3).

2. You shall not make for yourself a carved image (Exod 20:4-5).

3. You shall not take the name of the Lord your God in vain (Exod 20:7).

4. Remember the Sabbath day, to keep it holy (Exod 20:8).

5. Honor your father and your mother (Exod 20:12).

6. You shall not murder (Exod 20:13).

7. You shall not commit adultery (Exod 20:14).

8. You shall not steal (Exod 20:15).

9. You shall not bear false witness against your neighbor (Exod 20:16).

10. You shall not covet (Exod 20:17).

Unit 5: The Exodus

Passage	Which Commandment?
Exodus 20:22-26	
Exodus 21:1-11	
Exodus 21:12-15	
Exodus 21:16	
Exodus 21:17	
Exodus 21:18-27	
Exodus 21:28-33	
Exodus 21:35-36	

2. Life Under the Law. Consider just the last day of your life in light of the requirements of the Law. How many times have you broken the Law? You probably have not committed murder or adultery in the last day, for example, but what about hatred, lust, covetousness? Write a paragraph explaining the ways you have broken the Law and which law is particularly hard for you. Then write a prayer of confession to the Lord. End by reading 1 John 1:9 and thanking God for His forgiveness. _____

_____
_____
_____
_____
_____
_____
_____
_____
_____
_____
_____
_____

3. Sing the Ten Commandments. Find a song version of the ten commandments online and learn to sing along with it. Sing through it on your own at least five times. Did you find it easy to memorize them through song?_____

EVALUATION

1. Who was God talking to in the first part of Exodus 20? _____
_____
_____

2. What was the first thing God said from the top of the mountain? _____
_____

3. Why is this first thing God spoke to the nation of Israel important? _____
_____
_____

4. What are the Ten Commandments? _____
_____
_____
_____

5. The sixth commandment says not to kill anyone, is there more to it than that when you work out the details? Explain. _____
_____
_____

6. Apply that same understanding to the other commandments. What about the seventh? The eighth? etc. _____
_____
_____
_____
_____
_____
_____
_____

LESSON 5.8

True Worship in the Tabernacle and False Worship of the Golden Calf

UNIT 5

THE STORY

Lesson theme - Idolatry always fails to deliver on its promises.

God's plan from the beginning was to create a place for His people to dwell with Him so that they could be incorporated into the life and fellowship of the Holy Trinity. The garden of Eden was to be this place of fellowship, but because of their sin, Adam and Eve were expelled from God's presence. The rest of the Bible is the Story of the reconciliation of God and man so that they can dwell in fellowship. The tabernacle was a portable garden of Eden for the nation of Israel, and through its layout, furniture and operation we get a picture of what it takes for man to enter into the presence of the almighty God. Proper worship is *always* re-entry into the dwelling place of God according to God's ordained means for doing so. False worship entails the creation of forms and images so that man can attempt worship with a false god on his own terms. But what man thinks he gains by worshiping false gods, he actually loses, since these gods lack the power to save him.

The tabernacle

After receiving the Ten Commandments, the Lord gave Moses instructions on how to prepare the tabernacle. From these instructions in Exodus 25-31 (and some parallel discussion in Leviticus 1-7), we get a clear picture of what the tabernacle would have looked like. Take a little time to research the layout of the tabernacle. Pay attention primarily to the similarities between the tabernacle and the garden of Eden (see lesson 1.4 in *The Beginning*).

OVERVIEW

Instead of having a face-to-face relationship with God, Israel chose to have a relationship with Him through the Law. However, God still desired to meet with His people, so He had them build the tabernacle, a portable Mt. Sinai and a miniature garden of Eden where God's presence dwelt in the Most Holy Place. There the people could truly worship the Lord through representative priests and sacrifices. However, when Moses descended from Mt. Sinai to call Israel to true worship, he found them worshiping a false god made of metal. This lesson is about the contrast between true worship and false worship.

SOURCE MATERIAL

- Genesis 2:8-17
- Ezekiel 28:11-15
- Genesis 3:22-24
- Exodus 25-34
- Psalm 15, 115
- Proverbs 9:10-12
- *Carta's Illustrated Encyclopedia of the Holy Temple in Jerusalem* by Israel Ariel, et al.

The first thing God told Moses about building the tabernacle was that he was to build it from the freewill offerings of the people. Specifically, God told Moses, "From everyone who gives it willingly with his heart you shall take My offering" (Exod 25:2). God wanted the tabernacle to be built with the "hearts" of people; anything

Unit 5: The Exodus

OBJECTIVES

Feel...

- the resonance between the garden of Eden and the tabernacle.
- joy that God was working toward restoring fellowship with His people.
- disgust at how quickly the people forsook Yahweh, pathetically exchanging the Maker of heaven and earth for a gold statue.

Understand...

- how and why the tabernacle looked like the garden of Eden.
- the overall layout and orientation of the tabernacle.
- the key difference between true and false worship.

Apply this understanding by...

- analyzing your own life to see where you are forsaking the power of God because of your false worship.
- repenting of any false worship and turning to the true and living God.

they gave freely from their hearts would be the materials for the tabernacle.

The layout of the tabernacle is significant. In Lesson 1.4 we saw a picture of the layout of the garden of Eden, with the garden on the east and the sanctuary of the Lord on the west. The river flowed down from the mountain and through the garden, then out to water the whole world. The tabernacle was laid out similarly with the Holy Place on the east and the sanctuary (known as the Holy of Holies or Most Holy Place) on the west. The tabernacle was a portable tent structure, so that wherever Israel went, they could worship the Lord. When it was set up, it was always oriented with the Most Holy Place on the west and the entrance on the east. In the same way, Adam and Eve were expelled from the garden into the land on the east; the entrance to the garden was, therefore, on the east, protected by an angel with a flaming sword.

The central piece of furniture in the tabernacle was the ark of the covenant. The instructions for its construction are given in Exodus 25:10-22. On top of the ark there was a platform called the mercy seat, and at each end of the mercy seat, facing the seat, was a golden cherub with their wings touching. The people were to place the covenant the Lord had made with them inside the ark. The purpose of the ark is what's really significant here: it was the throne of God. God said, "And there I will meet with you, and I will speak with you from above the mercy seat, from between the two cherubim which are on the ark of the Testimony, about everything which I will give you in commandment to the children of Israel" (Exod 25:22). The ark was to be placed in the Most Holy Place.

A table overlaid with gold was placed on the north side (right side upon entering the tabernacle) of the Holy Place (Exod 26:35). This table was called the table of showbread, because the bread was placed on the table in the presence of the Lord; it was shown to Him. Each Sabbath, the priests would enter the Holy Place and eat the bread in the presence of the Lord which represented sharing a meal with God and eating in His presence. The symbolic significance being that God *wants* to share a meal with His people. Across from the table of showbread, on the south (left) side of the tabernacle was the golden lampstand (Exod 26:35), which had seven branches, each designed to look like almond branches (Exod 25:31-37). The lampstand provided the only light in the tabernacle (apart from the glory of the Lord). Its appearance as a tree reminds us of the garden of Eden which the entire Holy Place represented. Finally, in the center of the Holy Place stood the altar of incense where the priests would burn sweet incense to the Lord, representing the prayers of the people.

The tabernacle was constructed of wooden poles and curtains (Exod 26:1, 15). You can imagine walking into the Holy Place and seeing wooden poles lining the sides from which the cloth would hang on the outside. You might even feel like you were in a garden with those wooden poles like trees and the golden lampstand standing as a tree in the middle of the garden. (A Jewish group in Jerusalem has reconstructed the golden lampstand to the specifications given in Exodus. Search online to see a picture, or use the illustrations in the Carta encyclopedia cited in the sources section.)

The court of the tabernacle was surrounded by a curtain-fence on all sides with the entrance to the tabernacle on the east (Exod 27:1). When entering the court, you would first come to the altar of burnt offering where the sacrifices were offered. If you were coming to the tabernacle to offer a sacrifice, a priest would cut up the animal as you entered; then it would be placed on the altar and burned. The animal represented the worshiper being cut up into pieces and consecrated for the presence of God. No one entered God's presence without dying. The same thing would have happened to re-enter the garden of Eden—you would have to pass the cherub guard who would cut you up and burn you with a flaming sword. Ultimately, Jesus died and we died with Him so that we can now enter into the presence of the Lord. All of this was imaged in the tabernacle.

Beyond the bronze altar, but before getting to the tabernacle itself, stood the bronze laver (Exod 30:17-21). Here, the priests would wash themselves, making themselves ritually clean. No one enters into God's presence without first being made clean.

The golden calf
After Moses received these instructions, he came down from the mountain, carrying the tablets inscribed with the Law. Here, he found Israel worshiping the golden calf (Exod 32). He reacted so strongly to their false worship, that he broke the tablets of the Law.

The usual when the story of the golden calf is taught, the focus is on how *quickly* the people deserted Yahweh. While Moses was still up on the mountain, just after they had heard the voice of God Himself speaking the Ten Commandments—including one against having other gods before Yahweh and another one against making carved images to worship—there they were, making a carved image to worship. The quickness of Israel's desertion of worshiping Yahweh is a valid point, but the main point you want to understand is the contrast between true and false worship.

True worship mirrors the order of the world established at Eden. The first obstacle between the worshiper and God was the angel with the flaming sword. Anyone who tried to pass would be cut in pieces and set on fire. Unable to approach God and live, the worshiper brought an animal in his place. He placed his hands on the animal's head to identify it with himself and then killed it. The animal was then cut in pieces and set on fire on the altar (Remember that the altar was a portable Mt. Sinai, complete with fire and smoke on top. The fire came directly from God out of the sanctuary [Lev 9:22-24].) And so on—

all the lessons taught by each of the pieces of tabernacle furniture are pointing to the fact that sinners need to be purified in order to approach God. You don't need to know all the details; the big lesson, when you add it all up, is that God is *huge* and powerful and hates sin and impurity. Approaching Him is a *big, big deal.*

Of course, the people hadn't heard the details of tabernacle worship yet and didn't know its symbolism. But they saw God descend on the mountain in fire and smoke, and they heard His voice speaking the Ten Commandments to them, and they were terrified. The false worship they chose was terribly shabby by comparison. In contrast to Yahweh's glory, which a mortal man couldn't see and live, the glory of the idol was nothing but the shine of polished gold. The god was a statue, made by Aaron's hands according to the people's will, displayed in full view. Instead of the worship-journey back into Eden, the people sat down to eat and drink and rise up to play before the golden calf. They cavorted before the idol without fear, *because it was so inglorious and impotent they had nothing to fear.* This was an idol that couldn't hurt them—but if it had so little power, how could it save them? They could lie about its history (Exod 32:4), but would they be able to rely on it in the future?

God took the matter of Israel's idolatry very seriously and sent Moses down to rebuke the people, destroy the idol, and judge the sin. Moses also took it very seriously—so much so that he shattered the stone tablets of the covenant and had the Levites kill 3,000 people who were involved in the sin (Exod 32:19, 27-28).

When Moses returned to the mountain, God wrote on a second set of tablets to replace the first set that Moses had broken (Exod 34:1-28). This constituted a renewal of the covenant (which was necessary, since the people had already broken what they committed to in Exod 19:8). By giving them the Law again, God was affirming that He still intended to hold up His end of the covenant, and He still expected them to hold up theirs.

When Moses returned to the people this time, they gathered the materials for the tabernacle, built it, consecrated the priests, and began to worship in the way that God had commanded.

APPLICATION

In America we don't usually worship golden calves, but that doesn't mean we don't fall into idolatry. To get a better look at our idols, ask yourself a series of questions:

- To what do I attribute my successes?
- To what do I attribute my deliverance from trouble?
- What am I afraid of?

The things we think of as giving us success or saving us from trouble and the things we are afraid of are the things we are tempted to make into idols.

Mocking the idol is one of the key biblical strategies for dealing with the idolatry in our own hearts. Psalm 115 provides a model for how to go about it. Psalm 15 gives the positive side—the sort of worshiper God is seeking.

Lesson 5.8

ACTIVITIES

1. Idolatry and Fear. Brainstorm about modern idolatry. In America, people don't usually worship golden calves, but what are people tempted to worship? Make a list on the left side in the space provided below (include things like "money", etc.). Then brainstorm about what people are afraid of. Make a list on the right side. Can these idols really save us from the things we are afraid of?

What People Worship Today	What People Are Afraid of Today

Unit 5: The Exodus

2. Journal Time: Fear. Think through the questions below and write down your answers in the space provided.

What are your greatest fears? _____
_____
_____
_____
_____

Do any of these fears provide temptation for some sort of false worship? If so, in what ways? _____
_____
_____
_____
_____
_____
_____
_____

Are you involved in false worship in any of these areas of fear? _____
_____
_____
_____
_____

Write a prayer repenting of any false worship and ask God to teach you how to worship properly in each area of your life in which you are afraid. _____
_____
_____
_____
_____
_____

EVALUATION

1. In what ways did the tabernacle reflect the garden of Eden?

2. Why did the tabernacle reflect the garden of Eden?

3. What is the key difference between true and false worship?

4. What's the key weakness of false worship?

LESSON 5.9

Priestly Law: God Separated Israel as a Nation of Priests

THE STORY

Lesson Theme - Living as God's people

God intended Israel to be a nation of priests, separated from the world, yet being a blessing to all peoples. In this lesson, we learn about the sacrifices, the holiness laws, and the feasts—the three things God gave Israel to keep them separate from the world and teach them how to relate to God.

The sacrifices

God gave Israel a whole set of sacrifices, and time doesn't permit us to look at all of them. But let's consider one particular offering that contained most of the elements of most of the offerings: the ascension offering. This was the offering made every morning and evening for the people and was also made by worshipers on certain occasions.

The Hebrew term that we are translating "ascension offering" is usually translated "burnt offering" (e.g., in Lev 1 and Exod 29). The word means neither "burnt" nor "offering"—it's from a root that means "to ascend" (hence our translation). Getting the language right is important here, because ascension was at the very heart of the meaning of the sacrifice.

When the worshiper approached to make an ascension offering, he first laid his hands on the animal's head, so that God would accept the animal on his behalf. Then, the worshiper (*not* the priest) killed and skinned the animal himself, washing its legs and entrails. The priests would take the blood and sprinkle the altar, then lay the

OVERVIEW

God intended Israel to have a priestly function to the nations of the world. To that end, He gave Israel special instructions to keep them separate from the other nations and to teach them how man relates to God. The sacrifices taught the lessons of the worship-journey back to Eden; the holiness laws maintained Israel's separateness, and the feasts taught a complex set of lessons about time.

SOURCE MATERIAL

- Exodus 29:38-46
- Leviticus, especially chapters 1, 11, 23
- Psalm 104

fire and wood in order on the altar and lay the entire animal out on the altar to be completely burned.

Remember that to the Israelites, God was not off in a nebulous "heaven" somewhere beyond the sky. God dwelt in the pillar of cloud by day and the pillar of fire by night, and that glory cloud hovered above the tabernacle for everyone to see. So as the worshiper watched, the animal—which, let us not forget, represented him—was completely consumed in the flames and ascended as smoke to the glory cloud above the tabernacle. The animal literally went up to the presence of God on behalf of the worshiper, while the worshiper watched.

Unit 5: The Exodus

OBJECTIVES

Feel...

- gratitude that it is no longer necessary to slaughter animals in order to enter God's presence.
- gratitude that all the holiness laws no longer apply to God's people.
- challenged that what visibly marks us today (love for each other) is much more difficult than Israel's marks of separation.
- gratitude for God's care of His people when He set out to make sure Israel got adequate rest.

Understand...

- the basics of the sacrificial system: the relations between worshiper, animal, priest and God.
- that the basic nature of holiness is not moral righteousness, but separateness-to-God.
- the basic nature of the holiness laws: they forced Israel to be *different* at every turn from the nations that surrounded them.
- the basic lesson of the feasts: all time belongs to God, and He wants us to spend quite a lot of it celebrating and resting.

Apply this understanding by...

- contemplating the enormity of what happens when you're in church: you are *in the presence of God*, and you don't have to die to be there.
- examining your own behavior to see if your love for others makes you visibly different from the world.
- appreciating the rest that you get in the course of a week.

There were a number of different types of sacrifice that differed in the details, depending on their purpose. But the essential lesson of sacrifice is that we cannot re-enter God's holy sanctuary without dying—without being cut in pieces and set on fire. If we want to survive an encounter with God, someone has to go in our place. In ancient Israel, the animal went instead of the worshiper, just like Abraham killed the ram instead of Isaac.

The morning and evening sacrifices offered on behalf of the people every single day (see Exod 29) were ascension offerings that incorporated not only an animal, but grain, wine, and oil—the basic staple foods in that time and place (see Ps 104, which celebrates all these things). These offerings continually purified the people. This is the reason why the holiness laws repeat the phrase "he shall be unclean until evening" about various things—see Lev 11, 15, 19 for numerous examples). The necessary washing or purification was carried out, and then the evening sacrifice made atonement for the impurity; after that, the person was clean again.

The holiness laws

Holiness laws were not principally about moral righteousness. Unrighteousness would make a person unclean, of course, but there were a lot of other things that could make a person unclean. Holiness—being ritually clean—is about being separated to God for His purposes. Since it was God's purpose to make Israel a nation of priests, He chose to give them a number of regulations that separated them from the other nations.

Among these regulations were the food laws, recounted in great detail in Leviticus 11. The unclean animals were not in any way inferior—God describes Jesus as a lion, for example, even though a lion was an unclean animal. But forbidding Israel to eat certain foods was one of the ways God chose to set Israel apart from the other nations. God also forbade sowing a field with mixed seed or wearing clothes with mixed fibers (Lev 19:19), so no poly-cotton clothing for an observant Jew. All these differences guaranteed that you could identify an Israelite on sight by his clothing, grooming, the way he farmed and treated his animals, and in countless other little ways.

The feasts
Leviticus 23 gives a succinct summary of the feasts, here are some of the highlights:

Notice that the Sabbath was a feast of the Lord. It was meant to be a feast, a day of rejoicing and rest, and God required that they observe it every single week. The Sabbath was not about what the Israelites *couldn't* do—which is often how it is taught—it was a festival day on which *work* was banned, and the people got to celebrate and rest.

The rest of the feasts recur annually. The feasts of Passover and Unleavened Bread commemorate Israel's escape from Egypt. Firstfruits celebrates the beginning of the harvest coming in. Weeks (Pentecost) is the beginning of summer and a celebration of the early harvest. Trumpets comes in the fall—the blowing of trumpets called the people to assemble for war or celebration. The Day of Atonement follows Trumpets; it is a fast rather than a feast, a day of mourning for sins. Tabernacles is the full harvest celebration.

The Israelites were to live in tents (tabernacles) during this feast to commemorate the time Israel spent wandering in the wilderness, but it was also a time to celebrate God's great provision—think of it as a week-long Thanksgiving feast.

The prophetic aspect of the initial four feasts has already been fulfilled: Christ is our Passover, who died without sin (symbolized by leaven) for us, and rose from the dead as the firstfruits of the resurrection. The Holy Spirit came on Pentecost, inaugurating the great harvest Jesus told us to pray for (Matt 9:37-38). Trumpets remains to be fulfilled when the last trumpet is blown to gather God's people to Him.

The Day of Atonement is, of course, also fulfilled in one sense—Christ has atoned for the sins of the world. However, the Day of Atonement focuses specifically on the deliverance of Israel from her sins, and the nation of Israel has not yet recognized her Messiah. She will, one day (see Rom 11:26).

The Feast of Tabernacles remains to be fulfilled when the fullness of the harvest begun at Pentecost has come in, when all God's people from every tribe, tongue and nation are gathered before Him.

Holidays are central to the life of any culture; what you celebrate tells you who you are as a people. Israel's holidays were designed to shape them into a certain sort of people—a people who feasted before God and understood His goodness to them.

Unit 5: The Exodus

APPLICATION

In all three of these areas—sacrifices, holiness laws, and feasts or holidays—we are doing the same things that Israel was doing. The deep reality of how God's people relate to Him is unchanged from that day to this. But today, we don't get the same set of visual and tactile cues that we used to get. This is like graduating from using a coloring book to just using a blank sketch pad; it is a move into maturity, and it takes maturity to handle it. Israel drew near to God through the sacrifices. We often think of animal sacrifices just as something we don't have to do anymore, but thinking that way misses the whole point. An Israelite who brought an animal for an ascension offering was tangibly coming before God's presence. In our time, we get fewer visual and tactile cues, but the reality has not changed at all. When you go into church to worship, remember that you are not simply gathering with God's people for donuts and teaching. When you begin to worship, the roof opens, the walls grow thin, and you are before the throne of God. You can do that without slaughtering a lamb because Jesus has gone before you and opened the way.

The holiness laws were designed to set Israel apart from the surrounding nations, to make them visibly different. Today, God's people don't have to exhibit the set of visible differences that God gave to Israel, but He still requires us to be visibly different. Jesus told His disciples that He expected people to be able to recognize us by our love.

The holiness laws were also designed to teach Israel that God makes distinctions. He made different sorts of people and different sorts of things in the world, and He wants His people to respect the differences He built into the world. All things are not the same to Him. One of the major battleground issues of our own day involves this same lesson. The controversy over same-sex marriage comes down to this question: "Does it matter if I love a man or a woman? Of course they're different, but does the difference matter?" To God, it does. To effectively reflect His image, He designed marriage to be one man and one woman.

Israel's feasts reveal what God wanted to ingrain in the consciousness of the nation: certain key moments in their history, His annual provision for their needs, and the future coming of the Messiah. Today, we are free to observe days or not, as long as we do what we do unto the Lord (Rom 14:6). Consider your own family's customs. What holidays do you not really celebrate? Which ones are particularly important to you? What do your celebration habits say about you?

You are free to celebrate or skip any holiday you like, so long as you are fully convinced to do so (Rom 14:5). But you are required to do it unto the Lord. Do you?

ACTIVITIES

1. Journal Time: Visibly Different. Back in Moses' time, you could identify an Israelite on sight—they wore certain clothes, only ate certain foods, rested every Sabbath, kept certain feasts, and so on. God doesn't ask us to do those things, but He does ask us to be different. Jesus said, "By this all will know that you are My disciples, if you have love for one another" (John 13:35). Answer the following questions.

Make a list of ways that others could tell you are a disciple of Jesus just by watching you live your life.

_____
_____
_____
_____
_____
_____

Do you love people in noticeable ways? How? _____
_____
_____
_____
_____

If you don't love people in noticeable ways, what can you do to change that? _____
_____
_____
_____
_____
_____
_____
_____

Unit 5: The Exodus

2. The Feasts. All the feasts that God prescribed for Israel point towards the Messiah. Some of the feasts' prophecies have already been fulfilled (e.g. Passover), and some will be fulfilled in the future (e.g. Trumpets). All the feasts point towards the Messiah. Think through each feast, what it prophesies, and if that prophecy has been fulfilled yet. Fill in the table below.

Feast	Feast's Prophecy	Fulfillment of the Prophecy
Sabbath		
Passover/Unleavened Bread		
Firstfruits		
Feast of Weeks (Pentecost)		
Feast of Trumpets		
Day of Atonement		
Feast of Tabernacles		

Lesson 5.9

3. Happy Holidays. List out the holidays we celebrate on the left below, and briefly sketch out what they mean on the right side. July 4th means that we're Americans, part of an independent country; Mothers' Day means we appreciate our mothers; etc.

The Holidays We Celebrate Today	What these Holidays Mean

Unit 5: The Exodus

Think about what it would mean to celebrate Israel's holidays instead—a whole set of days throughout the year that point to Jesus. Write a paragraph below explaining how life would be different if you were to celebrate those holidays instead of ours.

EVALUATION

1. What is the principal lesson of the sacrifices? _____

2. Do we still need someone to go for us? _____

3. What is the principal lesson of the holiness laws? _____

4. As Christians, do we have holiness laws today? _____

5. What was the principal lesson of the feasts? _____

LESSON 5.10

Israel's Rebellion at Kadesh Barnea

UNIT 5

THE STORY

Lesson Theme - We cannot thwart God's victory, but we can fail to share in it.

After the completion of the tabernacle at Sinai, God's glory cloud lifted and began to lead Israel away from the mountain (Num 10:11). As they departed, Moses invited his Midianite brother-in-law, Hobab, to come with them. Hobab was inclined to return to his homeland in Midian, but Moses asked him and his people to come with Israel as scouts. (Remember that Midian was a son of Abraham by Keturah, the wife Abraham took after Sarah's death; so the Israelites and Midianites were distantly related through Abraham—see Gen 25:1-6.) And so they began to journey toward the land of Canaan (Num 10:29-33).

Note also what Moses said every time they took up the ark of the covenant: "Rise up, O LORD! Let Your enemies be scattered, and let those who hate You flee before You" (Num 10:35). These words were the inspiration for David's later composition in Psalm 68 (we'll return to this topic when we cover David).

The tale of the quail in Numbers 11:4-35 fits into the story as a continuing indication of the exodus generation's poor character. God had indirectly begun warning the Israelites that they needed to stop complaining back at the Red Sea (see Exod 15:26). They continued to complain, and the quail story was just the latest instance. God rained bread from heaven for them every day, and they couldn't appreciate the miracle; they just had to find something to gripe about. So God told them He would give them meat

OVERVIEW

God brought Israel to the borders of the promised land and prepared them to go in. Israel, still doubting God's good intentions for them, refused to enter the land; and so God allowed the people their choice—to die in the wilderness.

SOURCE MATERIAL

- Numbers 10:11-14:45
- Psalms 95, 106
- Proverbs 1:28-33
- Hebrews 3:7-19

"until it comes out your nostrils and becomes loathsome..." (Num 11:20). There's commentary on this tendency to gripe in Psalm 106 (see Ps 106:15 in particular).

The incident with Aaron and Miriam opposing Moses is noteworthy in a couple of respects (Num 12:1-15). First, it's an outstanding example of dodging the real issue. Aaron and Miriam were actually upset with Moses because of his choice of a wife. However, when they spoke, they didn't attack his choice of a wife; they attacked his office as leading prophet. This was dishonest; it didn't address what they were really concerned about and made resolving the conflict that much more difficult. Meanwhile, Aaron and Miriam had also offended God, because God had chosen Moses to lead. God became angry with Aaron and Miriam; He addressed the problem

83

Unit 5: The Exodus

OBJECTIVES

Feel...

- admiration for Joshua and Caleb for standing up to overwhelming pressure from the other ten spies and the people.
- disgust that the people of Israel still didn't trust God after all that He had done for them.
- surprise and disbelief at the people's stubbornness at trying to invade the land after God had judged them and it was too late.

Understand...

- that God had repeatedly demonstrated His grace and goodness to Israel, but they still didn't trust Him.
- that the exodus generation cursed itself, and the curse came to pass—the whole generation died in the desert.
- that repentance is always welcome when we've sinned, but some consequences can't be avoided.

Apply this understanding by...

- identifying areas in your own life where you are being called upon to trust and obey God.
- seeking to act on God's call immediately, not delaying obedience.

very directly and inflicted Miriam with leprosy (Num 12:9-10). Moses responded with love and mercy for his sister, and she was healed. We've already had a good look at Aaron's weaknesses in the golden calf incident; now we see that Miriam had her failings as well. The entire generation, even the leadership, was willing to rebel at pretty minimal provocation.

God led the people into the Wilderness of Paran, at Kadesh Barnea, and had them camp there at the borders of Canaan. At God's instruction, Moses sent twelve spies—one from each tribe—to spy out the land (Num 13:2). The spies returned and gave their report in front of all of Israel. The land was good and its fruit was abundant, they said, but the inhabitants of the land were mighty—there were giants there, and Israel would not be able to take the land (Num 13:27-28). Caleb opposed them, calling on Israel to go up at once and take the land, but the people refused to hear him (Num 13:30).

The people complained and mourned all night; note the substance of their complaint in Numbers 14:2-3. They were afraid God couldn't take care of them, and they would die in their attempt to take the land. It is crucial to understand that because of their behavior, they were cursing themselves, and God would respond to it. Joshua and Caleb tried to encourage the people, and notice how their encouragement was framed: God favors us, Joshua and Caleb said, and the people of the land have no protection. Let's not rebel against God; let's go and take the land (Num 14:7-9). The people responded by trying to kill Joshua and Caleb! But God intervened by bringing His glory cloud down to the tabernacle to meet with Moses (Num 14:10).

God spoke to Moses of killing the people and starting over, but Moses pleaded with God to have mercy on them. God responded with what amounts to a compromise: this generation that had persistently rebelled against Him would die, and their children would go in and inherit the land. The sole exceptions were Joshua and Caleb, because they were ready to obey the Lord (Num 14:11-24).

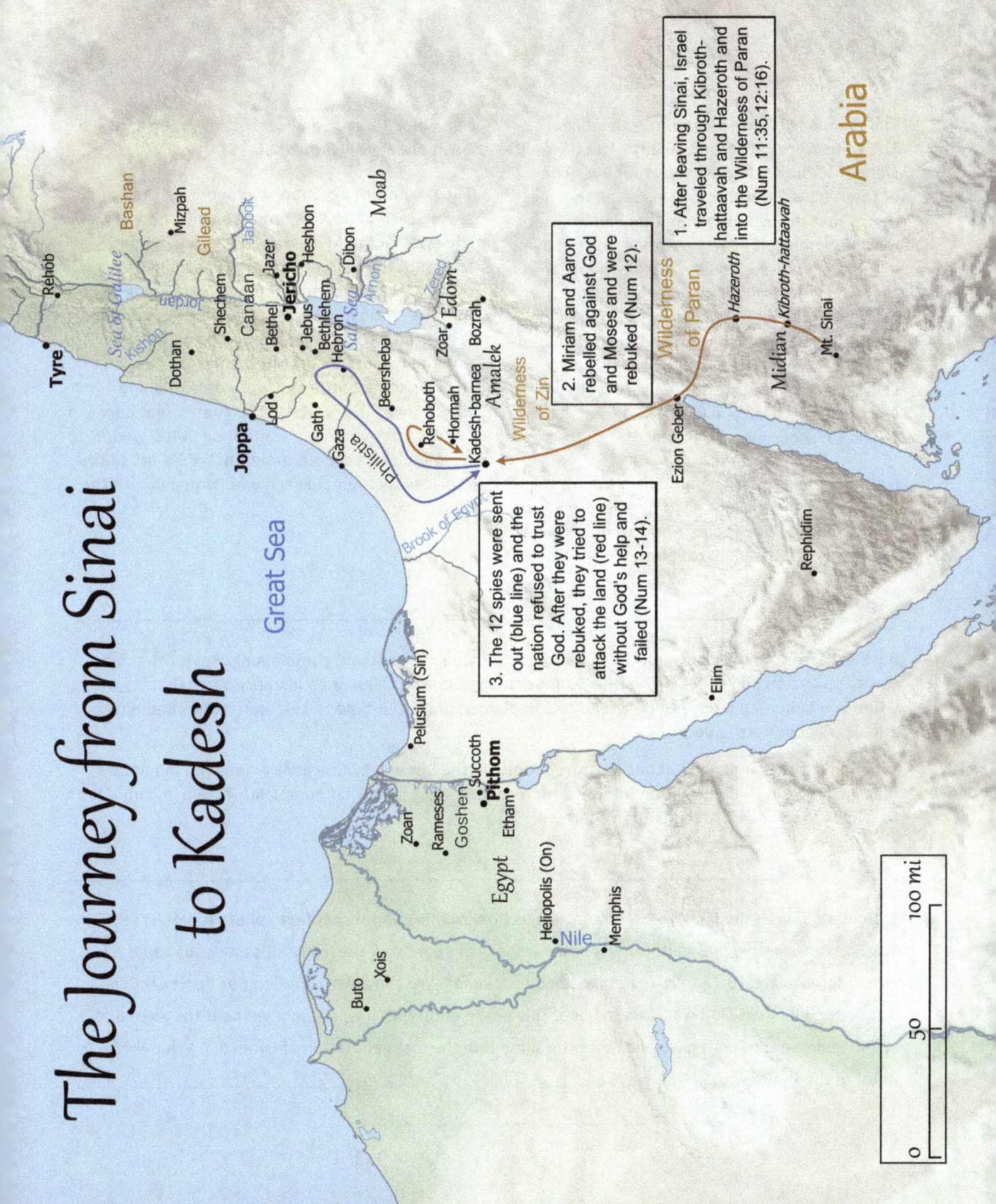

The manner of God's judgment is significant. The spies were in the land 40 days; Israel would wander in the wilderness a year for every one of these days. Over those 40 years, all the evil things that the exodus generation had accused God of planning for them—wandering and dying in the wilderness—would happen. They feared that God would kill them, when every day God was feeding them miraculously and delivering them from danger; God had had enough. Essentially, He said, "Fine; if you insist that I'm going to kill you in the wilderness, then very well—your will be done. I'll kill you in the wilderness" (Num 14:28-32, especially verse 28).

Not only that, but as an immediate sign of the coming judgment, God sent a plague and immediately killed the ten spies who had discouraged Israel and led them into rebellion. Only Joshua and Caleb remained alive, because they had been obedient (Num 14:36-38).

The next morning, Israel was suffering from a severe case of buyer's remorse. They now saw the error of their ways, and they didn't want to accept the judgment that was coming. They decided they had repented and were going to go into the land after all. Moses warned them that it was too late; God was not going with them, and they would be defeated. But they persisted in going up to battle and were defeated and driven away (Num 14:40-45). That defeat began Israel's forty-year-long wandering in the wilderness while the exodus generation died off, to be replaced by their children who would inherit the land.

APPLICATION

Back in Lesson 5.5, we considered the difference between lament and complaining. Revisit that lesson's application and check up on how you are doing. Can you think of an instance since that lesson when you lamented before God instead of complained? Take the time to celebrate your obedience and God's goodness to you.

What have you complained about most frequently in the last week? Consider where you might be failing to trust in God's provision for you with respect to that particular complaint. Take a few minutes to take that issue before the Lord in a lament.

ACTIVITIES

1. Read or Sing Psalm 95. This psalm teaches us how to think about that first generation of Israel. They are an example of unfaithfulness and hardness of heart; and these are sins any of us could fall into. 1 Corinthians 10:12 tells us to take heed lest we fall. We can always harden our hearts and miss out on the blessings God wants us to have. This psalm ends with a warning: if we hear His voice and yet still harden our hearts, we will meet the same fate the first generation of Israel did. What is the point of the Psalm ending that way? _____

2. Journal Time. Israel didn't obey God and go into the land when He told them to, but they did attack the land once it was too late, and were soundly defeated. Israel's experience teaches us that sometimes obedience is too late and has its consequences. Answer the following questions in the space below.

What things is God asking you to do or what things has He asked you to do in the past? _____

What happens when you delay doing these things? _____

Have you ever tried to do something too late and had to suffer the consequences? _____

Unit 5: The Exodus

3. God's Provision. God had been nothing but faithful to the Israelites, despite their failures. In the space below, make a list of all the things God had saved Israel from up to this point, starting with the plagues in Egypt.

Had God done anything that would justify Israel's distrust?

Lesson 5.10

EVALUATION

1. Did Joshua and Caleb have to stand up to the people?

2. Was it worth it for Joshua and Caleb to stand up to everyone else?

3. Whose idea was it for the exodus generation to die in the wilderness?

4. Was it right for Israel to belatedly obey and try to invade the land after all?

www.ingramcontent.com/pod-product-compliance
Lightning Source LLC
Chambersburg PA
CBHW081339080526
44588CB00017B/2673